MAISON THERAPY

MAISON

NEW HORIZON
PUBLICATIONS

Therapy

ALASTAIR SIMPSON

Illustrations by the Author

Published in Great Britain in 1993 by
New Horizon Publications
P.O. Box 7
Camberley Surrey GU15 1UD

ISBN 0 952 07580 6
British Library Cataloguing-in-Publication Data
A catalogue record for this book is
available from the British Library

Origination by Litho Link Ltd., Welshpool, Powys
Printed in England by Biddles Ltd., Guildford

For Barbara

who enjoyed it all a lot more than she thought she would

Contents

Introduction

I used to be normal; well at least normal in the sense that I acted like most of my colleagues at work. I seldom took my full vacation allowance and when I did go on holiday it took me so long to unwind that it was time to come home again. I suppose I suffered from some sort of stress.

Then suddenly everything changed.

I am still doing the same job and the pressure of business is the same or possibly even greater than before. Now I can't get enough vacation and the problem is switching on again when I return to work.

What has caused this sudden transformation?

I simply bought a house in France. Not a villa at the seaside or anything like that. That would not have done the trick. I bought an old house in a small village pretty much off the beaten tourist track.

Now, as soon as I come back from vacation, I am planning the next one which is never more than three months ahead. What will we take down with us in the car? What work will we do on the house when we are there?

Instead of having one holiday a year I am having four. My work does not seem to be suffering because of my more frequent absences, in fact, quite the reverse. In terms of vacation entitlement I am not unfair to the company but, for the first time in my business career, I am very fair to myself. I go abroad on business fairly frequently and often travel on a Sunday, so that I can meet with people first thing Monday morning. Now when I do this I take a half-day off in lieu. Days off in lieu have contributed substantially to the renovation of my house.

I am sure that there are many areas of France where one could buy a house and have the same happy experience that we are currently enjoying. We just happened to choose the Languedoc. Where is the Languedoc? Head down the Autoroute du Soleil from Lyons towards Marseilles. If you hang a left you are in Provence; if you hang a right and head towards Spain you pass through the Languedoc. It is very similar to what I have seen of Provence but not quite as fashionable and therefore not as expensive; you could call it the poor man's Provence. It also has long sandy beaches that, even in August, do not become overcrowded.

Eating too much and drinking to excess is undoubtedly bad for your health. But then so is stress. I eat very well on my frequent visits to France. I also take full advantage of the very good inexpensive local wines and to be sociable I partake of the odd Pastis. I must confess that I am developing quite a taste for being sociable. The important thing is not to feel guilty about such overindulgence because that will create stress. If you have just completed a couple of hours of hard physical labour on your house there is little chance of feeling guilty about such excesses - believe me.

Some people want to live in France full time. They just pack up and go. I am not so adventurous and anyway all I really want is a slice of the good life on a regular basis. I also want to continue to enjoy some of the things that England has to offer; like regular meetings with my children and granddaughter, good beer and a betting system on horse racing that I can understand.

My message is a simple one. A *maison de campagne* can be good for your health. This book is a light hearted account of our experiences. It relates the trials and tribulations of dealing with French estate agents, lawyers, the PTT and last, but not least, the local *Mairie*. You do not have to be a fluent French speaker although a smattering of the language certainly helps. There are a few potential pitfalls but they are very shallow and usually have an amusing side to them.

ALASTAIR SIMPSON

CHAPTER 1

Cirques and Grottes but Pas du Fromage

It all began when my company asked me to attend a seminar in Nice. I decided to take my wife, Barbara, with me so that we could have a little touring holiday after all the business sessions had been completed.

We were not too familiar with the South of France. When the children were much younger we had gone on holiday to Argelès, near the Spanish border. It was a camping holiday but it was camping without pain. The tent was already erected for you and there were proper beds to sleep on.

The previous few years we had gone camping halfway down the Atlantic coast of France. We had always enjoyed good weather but for some strange reason decided to take no chances this time and go further south to be absolutely sure of plenty of sunshine. It rained for twelve days out of fourteen in the middle of July.

My only lasting recollection of that holiday was the amusement we caused the other campers who were either British or, at least, understood English. Tents are very thin and, therefore, have no real soundproofing. You tend to forget this at times.

There were beds in the tents but no pillows and I like a pillow. Barbara had brought her little pillow that she always takes with her on holiday so she was all right. After about a week I started complaining that she should at least share the pillow with me. My whispered whingeing reached the stage late one night when she got fed up with me and, forgetting where we were, shouted, 'All right, you can have it tonight but not for the rest of the holiday.'

This exclamation probably did not quite reach the other side of the camp site but I reckon that a good fifty people were within earshot.

The rest of the holiday I was met with winks or looks of commiseration every time I passed anyone in my wanderings around the site.

This time the weather was perfect.

The Sunday Times colour supplement had published an article on touring in France and had recommended various routes. We had decided to opt for Tour 5 which would take us to the Cévennes and Haut Languedoc. This route started just north of Montpellier so we made our way slowly in that direction, stopping off at various Provençal seaside resorts en route. As it was still well before the major influx of tourists from the north the hotels were not too busy and we could be selective. Our choice was always strongly influenced by the contents and price of the menu that was displayed outside the hotel. The accommodation was always a secondary consideration. When I stayed in Paris hotels on company business I would pay 1000 francs a night for the room and around 200 francs for an evening meal. This ratio of 5 to 1 was not exactly reversed when it came to touring at my own expense but it was certainly altered. We would often find that the cost, per head, for the evening meal was more than the cost of the double room. The accommodation was not always great but you seldom noticed the deficiencies if you had dined well and sampled sufficient of the local wines.

As we were passing close to Arles we thought that we would stay overnight and have a look at the Roman Coliseum. In retrospect it was a mistake to try to introduce a bit of culture into what had been, up till that point, simply an exercise in eating, drinking and relaxation because it was there that I lost my new trousers and a bird did the unspeakable on Barbara's head. I suppose losing one's trousers is not too serious; after all Van Gogh lost an ear in Arles.

I am sure that lots of people have lost their trousers in many diverse and interesting ways. All I did was leave my new trousers in the wardrobe of the hotel and by the time I discovered the loss it was much too late to consider returning for them. I remember the hotelier well.

He was about my size, of a very happy disposition, and distinctly scruffy. I had no doubt that he would lay claim to the trousers and, for a short time, his appearance would improve until dropped cigarette ash and spilt red wine took their toll.

Barbara's experience was a little more exciting. We were on a large roundabout on the outskirts of Arles and I was awaiting instructions from my navigator as to which exit to take. I had already gone round the roundabout once and French roundabouts are dangerous places simply because the French cannot understand the general principal – if you are about to leave the roundabout it is best to be in the outside lane. Add to this the fact that the French have changed the right of way on roundabouts in recent years. The driver entering the roundabout used to have priority. Now it is the driver on the roundabout – a fact that has totally escaped many of the older drivers in rural areas. I recently had a stand off situation with an old French farmer in his ancient car. He stopped in the middle of the roundabout by our local supermarket to let me come on but, determined to teach him the proper rules, I stayed put. In the end, of course, I was the one who gave in when it became apparent that he would stay there all day if necessary to teach these stupid foreigners the rules of the road.

'Which exit?' I inquired politely of Barbara.

'*Merde*,' shouted my navigator feeling her head.

'There is no exit to Merde,' I said as I started my second circuit of the roundabout.

'Which exit?' I asked again, with only the slightest hint of impatience in my voice.

'A bird has just done a pooh on my head,' Barbara said half in complaint and half in amusement.

'I don't care,' I shouted, 'Which exit?'

'Either it was a very large bird,' she surmised, as she continued to wipe her hair, 'or it was a small bird that has not been very regular of late.'

'*Stuff the bird*,' I screamed, on my third circumnavigation of the roundabout, '*Which exit?*'

'I would gladly do so had I the chance,' she replied, 'and you can take the road to St. Gilles.'

Having got my instructions, I relaxed a bit and considered the fine piece of precision bombing that had just been executed through the relatively small aperture of the sunshine roof, especially as it was a moving target. It is one of these strange things but it never occurred to me for a moment that it could have been purely accidental.

I can quite easily imagine the scene. *Pierre le Pigeon* is flying along with a couple of his chums observing the scene below. There are not too many cars about, as it is fairly early in the morning, but they do notice the car with the open sunroof.

'*C'est n'est pas une voiture française*,' says Pierre to his flying companions.

They dip their wings in agreement as they know that no self-respecting Frenchman would risk polluting his Gauloise filled atmosphere with fresh air at such an early hour.

On closer inspection Pierre sees that it is an English car.

'*C'est dommage*,' he says, 'I would have preferred a German car but the English will do.'

'Look,' says one of his chums, 'they are approaching the roundabout. That is when to strike. Go for the driver and remember that he sits on the other side in an English car.'

'*Non*,' says Pierre, who had been carefully observing the scene below. 'We are not animals. We do not want to cause an accident even if they are English. The passenger is reading the map and giving directions. *Regardez*. I will hit the map on exactly the spot where we are at this moment. That will impress them.'

Pierre takes careful aim and drops his bomb. Just then the passenger leans forward for a closer look at the map.

'*Merde*,' shouts Pierre, as he sees his bomb land on the hair of the passenger.

'*Merde*,' shouts the passenger as she feels her hair.

Montpellier is a university town. We know this well because we always get lost in Montpellier and end up by the university. On this, our first occasion, we were fortunate in finding a garage where the attendant spoke excellent English and we were soon on our way towards the start of Tour 5.

Our first stop was St Martin de Londres. The *Londres* in the name apparently has nothing to do with London. I am told that a *londres* is a sort of otter-like animal.

We strolled up through the narrow lanes near the church and discovered a very nice little hotel hidden away in the cloisters. It looked very peaceful as there was no way that any traffic noises could reach this part of the village. The only problem was that it was closed or, rather, it was unmanned. On the door there was a telephone number that you had to ring to make a booking.

We found a telephone box on the main road opposite the *café* and rang the number. No answer. We tried another couple of times with the same result. We decided that some refreshment was in order so we wandered over to the café and discussed the situation with the patron over a cold beer. He said that he would try to get the number for us. He got the same result.

'This is often the case,' he said. 'Sometimes they are there. Most times they are not.'

Every five minutes he would go over to the phone and try again. Each time he would turn and shrug. After my third beer I decided that enough was enough and we pressed on.

We were impressed by the *Cirque de Navacelles* but I think we approached it from the wrong direction. I have visited it again since without having had such a nerve-racking journey.

We followed the signs and when we turned off the main road we found ourselves on a narrow road that wound forever upwards.

'I hope we do not meet anything coming down,' I commented.

'Perhaps it is a one way road.' Barbara said.

Just then a Renault 5 GTI hurtled round the bend ahead and bore down on us at around 100 kph. I did what I always do in situations like that. I relied upon the skill of the other driver to avoid a catastrophe, and as usual the other driver rose to the occasion, but I think in this case his skill was tested to the limit.

When we eventually reached the top we were on a plateau that was the southern end of the *Massive Central*. It was a very strange feeling having driven upwards for so long and then to drive for miles and miles over absolutely flat countryside.

We followed the signs for the *Cirque* and after a time came upon some parked cars and several people leaning over a wall. When we joined them we found ourselves looking into a great hole in the ground with a little village at the bottom. It really was a most unusual sight.

'I am glad that we made the effort,' I said to Barbara. 'I would not have liked to miss this, even though the roads were a bit precarious.'

'Good,' she said. 'As we are here we may as well go down and up the other side.'

There was no point in arguing. I looked at where the road wound down into the *Cirque* and resigned myself to another hair-raising experience. I am not a nervous driver but, unlike Paris taxi drivers, I do not know the width of my car down to the last millimetre.

It was not too bad on the way down. It was when we started up the other side and came to the sign that read, '*ROAD NARROWS – DANGEROUS BENDS* ', that I felt a slight twinge of apprehension. Could the road really get narrower? Could the bends become more acute? The answer was yes, but despite this we managed to find our way to the top on the other side.

The *Grotte de Demoiselles* was also well worth visiting. The *grotte* got its name because one of the stalagmite formations was supposed to resemble the Virgin and Child. They advised you to take a sweater with you as it got pretty cold inside but when you are standing in 90 degree heat you think something a little cooler will be nice.

Take a sweater with you.

Barbara and I followed the group through the *grotte* moving from one gallery to another, each one more impressive than the last. Eventually we came upon the formation that had given the *grotte* its name.

'This must be it,' Barbara said.

'Yes,' I agreed, 'It really does look like a statue of the Virgin and Child.'

Some of the other visitors who overheard our conversation had a look and nodded their agreement.

In the next gallery we came to the real Virgin and Child formation and this time there was absolutely no doubt. The other visitors gave us withering looks, as if to say – 'Of course, we did not really believe that it was the other one.' The main gallery is absolutely huge and it has been named The Cathedral. Apparently they hold midnight mass there at Christmas which must be quite a moving experience.

The disappointment for us was *Montpellier le Vieux*. This is not, as you might expect, an old ruined city, but rather a lot of different shaped rocks lying in a valley. The rocks all have the names of the objects that they are supposed to resemble. All I can say is that whoever named them had a very fertile imagination. The elephant, I suppose, could have looked like an elephant that had decided to lie down with his back to you. *Montpellier le Vieux* might have had more of an impact if strangely shaped rock formations were an unusual sight in that area but we had already passed several on our way there.

Not only was *Montpellier le Vieux* pretty dreadful, it was also a very long hike across some pretty rough terrain. I could not believe it when I saw bus loads of old age pensioners arriving. There was no way that they would make it even a quarter way round.

We never did find the *Roquefort* cheese caves. We followed the signs for a long way then the signs began to point in the direction that we had just come from. We decided to give the caves a miss and I cannot say that I was bitterly disappointed. I once visited the cheese warehouse at the Scottish Cooperative Wholesale Society in Glasgow and it was an olfactory experience that I had no wish to repeat.

The only other thing of consequence that happened was that Barbara got very bad bout of diarrhoea. This lasted for a few days and so we felt that a visit to the pharmacy was necessary.

The word for diarrhoea in French is the same as in English but is obviously pronounced very differently. Having failed to make ourselves understood we resorted to sign language - we held our stomachs and made faces and were given indigestion tablets. In the end we got the real thing and like most products sold by French pharmacies it was incredibly effective.

I hope I will not have to attempt to pronounce diarrhoea again in French and I also hope that I never have a problem with my car that requires any mention of the tyres. The French for tyre is *pneu*. I have tried pronouncing *pneu* whilst looking in the mirror. It is just not possible to do so and keep a normal facial expression.

CHAPTER 2

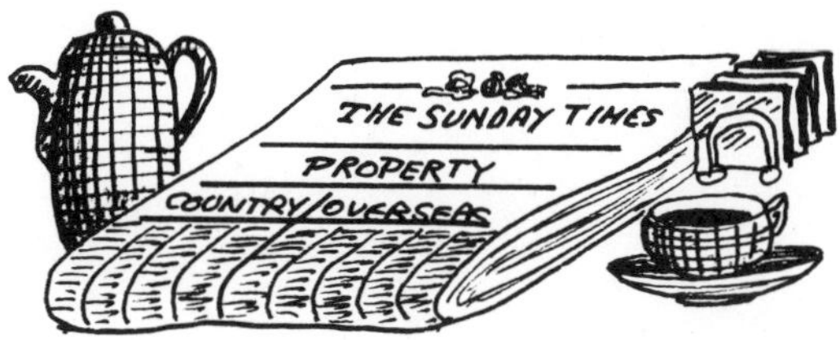

The Germ of an Idea

There is a pub, not a million miles from Kew Bridge, that serves the best pint of draught Bass to be found in the Greater London area. I will not mention the name, as part of this pub's charm is the fact that the superb quality of the Bass is known only to a discerning few and, for this reason, it is seldom crowded. Also I am not convinced that Tim, the landlord, could cope with sudden fame.

My first pint, since arriving back from France, was sitting, untouched on the table in front of me. I wanted to savour the moment a little longer.

This does not mean that I have anything against French beer. On a hot day, served ice cold, it certainly has its place as an acceptable form of refreshment. It is also incredibly cheap if you buy it in the supermarket in the small 25 cl bottles. My son-in-law had christened the little bottles 'dumpies'. The great thing about dumpies, besides being cheap, is that their size confuses wives. At home the plaintive cry of 'that is your fourth pint of beer today!' is not replaced, in France, by 'that is your seventeenth dumpie!' If there are murmurs of disapproval you merely point out dumpies are only a quarter of a pint in volume (an approximation rather than a falsehood). You add that French beer is a different strength from British beer, which is the truth, and if your wife takes this to mean that French beer is weaker then . . .

Ten seconds of savouring was quite long enough.

DRAUGHT
BASS

'Cheers,' I said to my fellow members of the Tuesday evening Bass Society.

Once a week, on a Tuesday evening, we would make the pilgrimage after work to the Bass pub. Why a Tuesday evening? Well it had originally been scheduled for Monday evenings as a means of recovering from the stresses and strains of returning to work after the weekend. Then one of our number, Fred by name, had announced that he wanted to do a Masters in Statistics at the local Polytechnic and the classes were on a Monday evening.

Our first reaction was, of course, to advise him to seek psychiatric help. At his age, such a qualification would hardly enhance his career prospects so it had to be a sort of penance resulting from his guilt complex.

Fred had, you see, worked for many years as a field engineer with the company and now found himself working in marketing. He felt in many ways that he had betrayed his roots as the engineering function, in our organisation, traditionally viewed marketing people with contempt. They considered them to be dishonest, idle and overpaid. Now that the ex-engineer had actually joined marketing he was disappointed to find only two of these accusations to be true.

When he ignored our well intentioned advice, we decided to review the list of classes available to him on other evenings. We made constructive suggestions but to no avail. His mind was set on statistics and all our pleas of a switch to more useful subjects such as advanced needlework were in vain. Monday evening became Tuesday evening.

There were six regular members of our group and all six of us were present that Tuesday evening.

It was unusual, on such occasions, to discuss anything related to work so I was a little surprised when someone asked me how the meeting had gone in Nice.

'Very well really,' I replied. 'Everybody seemed happy. The weather was good. The Americans added substantially to their Air Miles. There was a gift; a nice little alarm clock. Business as usual really. It also paid for me to get down there to start my holiday.'

As touring in France, particularly with emphasis on food and drink, was an acceptable subject for discussion I proceeded to give them an account of my holiday. I gave brief details of my route and made a particular point of saying how impressed I was with the area to the north and west of Montpellier.

'There are all these picturesque little villages surrounded by vineyards,' I said. 'You can go a few kilometres further from the coast and you are in the hilly region which is very scenic with its river gorges, or you can drive for half an hour and get to a nice spacious Mediterranean beach. It would be an ideal place to buy a little holiday home,' I concluded.

'I know,' David, one of our number said. 'I have a house in that area.'

This came as rather a surprise to us as he had never mentioned it before. Now that I own a property there myself I can understand why. Once it becomes known that you have a house abroad casual acquaintances suddenly become old friends and there is no shortage of people who are willing to go out of their way, whilst on holiday, to go and spend a week or so checking that all is in order with your property.

David went on to explain the exact location of his house.

'You must have passed very close to it on your travels,' he said.

I told him the route that we had taken and, indeed, at one time we were only a few kilometres from his village and right in the middle of the area that I particularly liked.

Until this moment the thought of owning a property in France had not entered my head but now I found myself asking David all sorts of questions. As it happened, Taff, another member of our little group, had also toured that part of France recently and was interested in the idea - he has a wife who works so he is under the constant strain of looking for ways to spend their substantial joint income.

David knew France well as he had worked for our company in Paris for several years. He was also a man of property, in fact, many properties and he always seemed to make a nice little profit when he disposed of them so here was a man whose advice was worth having.

'Now is the time to buy,' he said. 'A few years ago when I bought my place there was very little on the market but now there are plenty of properties for sale and they are not expensive.'

'So what has changed?' I asked.

'The Government. Under the Socialists the French, particularly the Parisians, did not have the spare cash to buy holiday cottages. But the Socialists will be defeated at the next election and then everything will change. So do not hang about. Buy now.'

If he had gone on to offer his own house for sale my suspicions would have been aroused but as he did not do so I concluded that he was giving us his honest opinion.

As it turned out, he was right about it being a good time to buy, but for the wrong reason. He was right, because the exchange rate at that time was 12 francs to the pound, but he was wrong about the Parisians rushing down to buy everything in sight and raising house prices after the election. Prices are still very reasonable and I do not think there has been more than a few percentage points rise in the last six years.

David said that the thing to do was to buy a village house. Taff and I agreed with him that we wanted to be inland – we did not want a new flat or villa on the coast but why not a house outside the village with a bit of land? That was OK, David said, if you were going to live down there all the time but if it was a holiday home you would run a high risk of finding it burgled if it was fairly remote. In a village the villagers look after your house for you. They all know when it is unoccupied and it is almost impossible for anyone to get into the house without the villagers being aware.

This all sounded very logical and Taff and I decided that we were both in the market for small, cheap, village houses, close to the hills but still within reasonable driving distance from the coast.

Now normally such a decision would have been induced by the draught Bass and quickly dismissed the following morning in the cold clear light of dawn. After all, I did not have any money. On the other hand I could always borrow a bit from the bank. We were not exactly talking about a fortune; probably something in the region of twenty to thirty thousand pounds. The mortgage on my house was quite small and if I borrowed, say, twenty-five thousand pounds, I would still be paying a lot less in house loans than most people on my income level.

The realisation that I was beginning to treat the idea of buying a property in France with a certain degree of seriousness suddenly reminded me of something. I had a wife. Perhaps I should give her a slight hint of my intentions before progressing any further along the road.

'You are thinking of doing what?' Barbara cried, giving me the same sort of look as when I had told her that I was going to invest our savings in gold.

I explained how I thought that we could afford the additional mortgage payments and how we would save money on holidays.

'You mean we are going to spend all of our holidays in the same place from now on?' she asked.

'Well, no,' I said. 'We can have other holidays as well.'

'Then how are we going to save money on holidays?'

'Well, perhaps we will not save any money on holidays, but we will be able to have more holidays if we have our own place.' I suggested.

This approach seemed to elicit a slightly less pessimistic response.

'I am not sure about this idea,' she mused. 'I don't want to spend all my time on holiday doing housework. A holiday is supposed to be a change.'

'It will only be a small house,' I said. 'A quick dust round once a fortnight will do the trick. Anyway the air is so clear in that part of the world that houses do not get very dirty.'

I was going to add that I would help with the housework but then I thought that I would save that for use as a last resort.

Barbara was still unconvinced but I could see that she was at least thinking about the idea.

'You did like the area,' I reminded her.

'Yes.'

'And I do get free petrol which is not really worth very much unless I do a lot of private mileage.'

'Yes.'

'And having a house in the South means that we are almost guaranteed sunshine for most of the year.'

'Yes.' Quite enthusiastic this time. Barbara likes the sun.

'So shall I investigate a bit further?' I asked.

'Well....'

'Are you sure that you are not letting the episode with the bird in Arles affect your thinking?' I asked.

'I can always wear a hat,' she said..

That weekend, I had a look at the overseas property page in the Sunday Times.

The first thing I did on the Monday morning was to go and find Taff.

'Do anything interesting at the weekend?' I enquired casually.

'Yes,' he said.

'What?' I asked.

Monday morning conversations in the office were often like this.

'I read the Sunday Times.'

'Did you by any chance have a look at the overseas property page?'

He gave me a piercing look. 'How did you know that?'

'Because I did the same,' I admitted.

'So when are we going to see this chap Singleton?' he asked.

'His office is just along the road in Richmond,' I said. 'Give him a call now and if he is free we will pop along at lunchtime.'

The Sunday Times had pointed us to a Mr. Singleton who, according to his advertisement, had a lot of French properties on his books. He was available to see us that lunchtime. We were not wasting any time.

Singleton turned out to be a very pleasant fellow and true to his advertisement he was able to supply us with several pages of properties in the region of our interest. He also sold us some large scale maps of the area at a very reasonable price. The visit certainly did nothing to dampen our enthusiasm and we took the name of his local agent with promises that we would call on him in the near future.

We now started to plan in earnest. As neither Taff nor I spoke much French we thought it would be a good idea to plan our visit to coincide with David's next vacation, as he was pretty fluent. There were one or two complications but the net result was that Barbara and I would go down first, stay a few days in an hotel in one of the main towns which I shall call Villegrande. David advised us that Villegrande would be a good centre for our house hunting. David and Lyn would arrive shortly afterwards and we would move in with them for a few days. About the same time Taff and his wife Melanie would arrive. They had selected an hotel very much off the beaten track. It looked quite interesting from the brochure so we had decided to join them there for the remainder of our holiday as we did not want to impose too much on David.

We had every intention of having a pleasant holiday but there was no doubt in my mind that I had, as my major objective, the purchase a property in the area.

CHAPTER 3

How Not to Open a French Bank Account

I left Paris en route for the South of France with a pocketful of 500 Franc notes; about three thousand pounds worth. This was somewhat more than the amount of cash that I normally carried around with me, being a dedicated plastic man.

I had been told that when you agreed to buy a house in France the estate agent asked you to sign a piece of paper that committed you to the purchase and you had to leave a ten per cent deposit. If you did not go through with the purchase then you lost your deposit.

The simple approach, of course, would have been to open a French bank account. Well, as it happens, I did open a French bank account. I went along to my UK High Street Bank and asked if they had any branches in France.

The lady I spoke to was very helpful. She consulted a large book and told me the locations of the small number of branches they had in France. There was a branch in Montpellier but, after due deliberation, I decided that a Paris branch would make more sense as I now visited Paris regularly.

As I was starting to make the arrangements a good six weeks before my departure date I assumed that there would be no problem.

All seemed to be going well. I asked my bank to transfer some money across to my new French account and they wrote to me saying that it had been done. I did not actually receive any acknowledgement from the Paris branch but perhaps that was normal.

It was about ten days before my departure date that I began to get worried because I had still not received my cheque book. I went to see the lady in my local branch who had been so helpful. She said not to worry because she would phone the Paris branch immediately and expedite matters.

I took a seat and watched the business of an average high street branch of a clearing bank being transacted. It is not often that I have this opportunity because I always use a cash dispenser. I think that cash dispensers are a marvellous invention, primarily because of the amount of time that you save, but also because I find that the machine can handle the delicate task of pointing out that you have insufficient funds with much more sensitivity than the average cashier.

The nice lady returned with a worried look on her face.

'They are very strange, these French banks,' she said. 'It would appear that they do not assume that you want a cheque book unless you specifically ask for one. They will place your order for a cheque book today but it will take at least a week for them to get it. Then they have to post it to you so it will probably take about ten days.'

I reviewed the situation. I could have been nasty to the nice lady but that would probably have made me feel worse as she was doing her best and opening French bank accounts probably did not figure too prominently on her training courses.

'The only way to ensure that I get the cheque book on time,' I told her, 'is for me to pick it up personally from the Paris branch.'

'I think that is the best approach,' she agreed. 'I will call them back immediately and tell them of your decision.'

I gave her the exact date that I would call in at the Paris branch and departed with a reasonable degree of confidence that everything would work out all right in the end.

We found the Paris branch quite easily.

A young man listened attentively whilst I explained the situation to him. I did not have much difficulty communicating with him as I had carefully rehearsed what I was going to say. The problem with rehearsing your speech beforehand is that it gives the impression that you have a greater command of the language than is actually the case.

This is fine if all goes to plan but if the scenario suddenly changes then you are in trouble.

When I had finished my little speech he asked me to wait a moment and went off to have a word with a somewhat older man sitting at a desk. I could see the older man shaking his head. This was a bad sign.

They both approached the counter. The older man began to talk to me very quickly accompanied by much waving of the hands. The younger man had moved a little to the side so as not to inhibit the gesticulations of the older man. He was obviously familiar with his style of communication.

I did not understand a word so I was forced to admit that I spoke very little French and could he please repeat what he said a little more slowly. At this point he stood back and guided the younger man to the opening in the counter. He addressed me in English.

He explained that this branch did not deal with any external accounts. My account must be at the other Paris branch.

'This is definitely the address I was given,' I said. I showed him the piece of paper with the address written on it.

He shook his head again. 'One moment,' he said. 'I will telephone our other branch and confirm that they have opened an account for you.'

We waited and watched. He started to nod his head, not at us, but at the person on the other end of the line. Things were beginning to look up.

'All is well,' he said when he returned. 'They have all the paperwork and an account has been opened in your name.'

'Good,' I said. 'Is the other branch near here?'

'No,' he replied. He got a map and showed us where it was. It was the other side of Paris. It would take us some time to get there.

'Do not go there immediately,' he said, 'because by the time you get there it will be closed for lunch.'

This was becoming a bit of a problem as the plan had been a quick in and out of Paris and an early start southwards. It was now going to be a late afternoon rather than a late morning departure.

At least I knew Paris well as I travelled there several times a month on business. I guided Barbara to the nearest Metro. I had already decided where we would have a spot of lunch on the way to the other branch.

Paris has an excellent rail transportation system which, I feel, must be subsidised to an incredible degree as they seem to do little to ensure that travellers actually pay their fare. First of all there is the famous Metro, where the barriers are just the right height for even a person of limited agility to clamber over. Then there is the RER, a sort of super Metro with fewer stops but covering many of the major locations such as La Defense, the business area, and Roissy, the station for Charles de Gaulle Airport. Finally there is SNCF, the French equivalent to British Rail, which I have found very useful when the Metro and RER are on strike. I often travel by RER to and from the airport rather than taking a taxi. Even though they do get quite crowded at times it is better to be moving than to be sitting in a traffic jam in a taxi. You also see a slice of Paris life when you travel by public transport.

It was on the RER, on the way to the airport, that I saw a little slip of a girl lay out a six foot male with the minimum of effort. We were just approaching the station before the airport so the train was not too crowded but there were still one or two people standing. I became aware that, just down the carriage, a slight altercation was taking place. It appeared that a man was smoking in a non-smoking area and a woman with a small child was taking exception to this. In the end she handed the child to a man behind her and pulled a small object from her handbag. Next thing I knew the offending male was out cold on the floor and a couple of people who had been standing near him were gasping for breath. The woman had a used a little spray can of CS gas with devastating effect.

The unconscious male apparently had not been on his own because two women now started to hit the anti-smoking campaigner with their handbags. The train drew into the station and the three women disappeared, locked in combat, along the platform. The man on the floor gradually regained consciousness and staggered off the train. The man who had taken the child, presumably the husband of the woman now fighting against superior odds, followed at a leisurely pace, apparently unconcerned by the whole episode.

You can buy these little spray cans of gas over the counter in France with no trouble at all. Considering the number of attacks against women in this country, I have often thought of buying cans for my wife and daughters, but I have resisted the temptation so far, as carrying such products is against the law in the UK. You can buy many things in

France that are very carefully controlled in this country. In the hunting season in France even the small local supermarkets have their shelves crammed with shotgun cartridges. If you want to rob a supermarket in France but you have no money to buy the cartridges this is no problem; you just smuggle your gun in and load up from the shelves.

I usually stay at the Hotel Scribe when I visit Paris on business. I like the hotel because it is not too large and it is well situated within a short walk of Auber, an RER station. I have stayed in the Hotel Scribe many times but had never picked up any hint that the hotel had a significant claim to fame. Then one day I bought a bottle of gin in the duty free shop at the airport and attached to the neck of the bottle was a little leaflet entitled *Famous Bars of the World*. I thought that a much travelled man, like myself, would have visited many of these bars but the only one that I had actually drunk in was the bar of the Hotel Scribe. Apparently, this hotel was used by war correspondents during the Second World War and it was from this hotel that the capitulation of the German nation was announced to the World. Just along from the Hotel Scribe, in the Rue Danou, is the famous Harry's Bar. They say that if you go there for a drink you will always meet someone you know, or at least see someone famous. I have yet to meet anyone I know, or recognise a famous person, on my visits to the bar but I must admit I do not go there often as the prices are pretty steep. On the other hand, I can understand why the bar has gained such a reputation. On one occasion, when I dropped in for a drink with a friend, a group of people got quite excited and began pointing at my companion as if they recognised him. Now I must admit that he did have a beard. Before I grew a moustache I only looked like me. Once I had the hirsute upper lip I was accused of resembling all sorts of people and, in many cases, the suggestion was none too flattering. I suppose a beard affords even more possibilities, especially after people have had a few drinks.

I took Barbara to a little restaurant I knew that offered good value for money. The sixty five franc menu included a fish dish, which pleased Barbara, and I could have *confit de canard*, one of my favourite dishes. Our mood soon improved. It was not the best *confit de canard* that I have ever tasted but it was perfectly acceptable and, it was after all a fairly modestly priced menu.

METRO
MENU
65F

The duck, in France, is used in the preparation of two main dishes which are frequently to be found on menus. First, there is *confit de canard*. This is the thigh of the duck which has been preserved in duck fat and it is always very tender meat. I am told that the proper way to cook it is to take a piece of duck and cover it in the fat. You put it in the oven on a grill and have a pan of chopped up potatoes, and possibly a few onions, underneath. As the duck is cooking the fat melts and falls on the potatoes and they are roasted to perfection. This is not a meal for the calorie sensitive diner. *Magret de Canard*, on the other hand can often be a relatively low calorie affair as it is seldom accompanied by such excellent potatoes. This is the breast of the duck which is roasted, sliced and served with a sauce. The sauce can vary tremendously as each individual chef has his, or her, own idea of the ideal recipe. I like my *magret de canard* to be *rosé*. However I seldom ask for it to be cooked in this way as the French idea of *rosé* can be very different from mine. I like the meat to be a delicate pink. I am sure, in some cases, where I have ordered *rosé*, in France that a distinct quacking sound has been audible from the plate.

We finished our lunch and made our way to the other branch of the bank in a much happier frame of mind. It was a young lady who greeted us this time and she spoke excellent English. She produced a computer listing and showed me the details of my account.

'Excellent,' I said. 'And now if you can let me have the cheque book we will not detain you any longer.'

'You do not have the cheque book?' She seemed surprised by my request.

The mood of bonhomie induced by the lunch was rapidly evaporating.

'No, I do not have a cheque book,' I said, in measured tones. 'I arranged to come in to see you today specifically to collect the cheque book.'

'But we have sent it to you in England,'

'Why?' I asked.

'Because that is normal procedure.'

'But I asked for the cheque book to be kept here for me to collect in person.'

'Who did you ask?' she enquired politely.

'The lady who deals with the foreign business in my local bank branch in England,' I said.

'Ah,' she responded with a raising of the eyebrows that indicated that the puzzle was finally solved.

'We were not informed, *Monsieur*.'

'Do you happen to have another cheque book?' I asked.

She shook her head.

In the end we decided that the only thing to do was to withdraw a sufficient sum in cash and hope that I was not mugged. This was duly done and I stuffed the notes into my least accessible pocket.

The account now did not have a great deal of money left in it so the young lady, in a very polite way, pointed out to me that in general they expected external account holders to maintain a credit balance of around twenty thousand francs. Now this, I thought, was a bit of a cheek. It reminded me of the time I was doing some work in a merchant bank in the City and shares were not too buoyant. The minimum that the bank would accept from a client was fifteen thousand pounds, a lot of money in the early seventies. Apparently some people who had invested the minimum amount looking for a steady growth in their fortunes now found that their holding was worth less than when they started. This in itself was bad enough but worse was to come when the bank wrote to them and said that if they did not invest additional funds to bring their holdings up to the minimum level the bank could no longer handle their business.

I pointed out to the young lady that the bank's performance, so far, had not been over-impressive and as I was planning to buy a house in France and would be transferring a large sum of money over I should probably be looking for a more efficient organisation. Anyway, I informed her, I saw no reason to keep more that a couple of hundred pounds in the account.

Her attitude changed dramatically on the mention of house purchase and large sums of money. You must, of course, remember that she worked in Paris and was probably thinking in terms of Paris house prices. She must have been very disappointed when the paltry sum eventually arrived and stayed for only a very short time before departing again.

I must admit that, after the initial problems, I have had very good service from the French branch but, in retrospect, it would probably have been better to open an account with a French bank with a countrywide network of branches.

Despite all the problems, I did at least get the French francs at a good exchange rate by transferring them across; much better than the tourist rate.

We were feeling a bit tired as we headed out of Paris because we had not slept much the previous evening.

A word about channel crossings. I live about an hour's drive from Portsmouth and, since the M25 opened, about two hour's drive from Dover. I used to think it was a good idea to book a cabin and travel the Portsmouth–Le Havre route. The trouble was, after doing this a few times, I suddenly realised how little sleep I was getting and how exhausted I felt the next day particularly when faced with a long drive.

Of course we did it all wrong. We would get on the boat, have a nice meal in the restaurant, chat to our fellow travellers and by the time we got into our bunk we only had about three hours before docking. We would then try desperately to go to sleep and seldom succeeded.

If you are going to travel this route the answer is to go straight to your cabin – take a hip flask if you require a nightcap as a trip to the bar can prove fatal. The only time I use the Portsmouth–Le Havre route now is when I have business in Paris as the drive from Le Havre is shorter and I can, in fact, arrive in Paris and be in the office before most of my French colleagues.

I now travel the Dover–Calais route almost exclusively because the autoroute has been extended right to the ferry port and I get a 50 per cent reduction from P&O Ferries whereas on the Portsmouth–Le Havre route I only get a 40 per cent reduction. If you buy a house in France you must buy P&O 5.5% Redeemable Non-Cumulative Preferred Stock. They were Townsend Thoresen when I first bought them. Six hundred shares at around a pound a share. It did not take me long, even with my limited business acumen, to decide that it was a good deal. I would save around a hundred pounds a trip and I planned to travel to France four times a year. In addition I would get my dividend of thirty-three pounds each year and my initial investment would still be worth what I paid for it. It is one of the few, in fact the only, wise investment that I have ever made in the stock market.

We did not travel too far that evening, leaving the autoroute around Joigny which is about 150 kilometres south of Paris, and finding a small hotel which was reasonably comfortable but had gone overboard with the French obsession for highly patterned wallpaper. Not only the walls and ceiling were papered but also the doors in the same violent design. I remember being woken in the first light of dawn by a strange sound. It was Barbara knocking her way around the walls trying to discover the location of the toilet door.

CHAPTER 4

Can This be a Typical French Estate Agent?

The next day we were really on our way. We had slept well and the next port of call, other than the odd stop for petrol and a snack, was the hotel in Villegrande.

The journey was fairly uneventful. We even sailed through Lyon which can often be a problem but this was a little late in the year for a major *bouchon*. A *bouchon* as you may have guessed is a traffic jam - a *tire bouchon* is a corkscrew - both very useful things to know.

We found the hotel without any difficulty. The hotel did not have a restaurant but David had given us a recommendation for dining that evening.

The restaurant was situated in a little square and, as it was a warm evening the tables were set up outside. We selected a table that would give us a good view of all that was going on in the square and settled down to enjoy our meal.

The meal was excellent. There was no *à la carte*, just the 80 franc menu which was not presented to you in written form. A waiter came along, told you what was on the menu and then waited to take your order. Now this made life a little difficult for the non-French speaker but we managed all right and it is really a very good system There was no dithering over the menu for ages before you make up your mind and because you did not want to keep the waiter waiting you sometimes ventured into the unknown but the food was always good and we were never disappointed.

We started with mixed *hors d'oeuvres*; ham and melon and *paté* and tomatoes, and then we had a choice of three dishes for the fish course (this was generally the best course) and a choice of veal or beef for the main course. The wine, which was included in the price, was a bit rough but not so bad that I felt obliged to ask for the wine list. It all added up to very good value.

At this stage you are probably wondering why I do not disclose the name of the town and the restaurant so that you too can sample the delights of the 80 franc menu for yourself. There are two sorts of restaurant that I mention in this book. There are the large restaurants who advertise, appear in guide books and even have magazine articles written about them. Then there are the small restaurants. I will name a large restaurant if my comments on it contain nothing but praise. On the other hand, if I am somewhat critical of the establishment then I will not identify it because I do not want to be sued. I will also not identify the small restaurants for purely selfish reasons. I generally only write about them if they are good and I do not want to be denied a table one lunchtime or evening because the restaurant has become too well known.

I will not name the restaurant in Villegrande because the last time we went there it had all changed. First of all we discovered that they now had a printed menu. The reason they needed a printed menu soon became apparent - there was no way that it could have been explained verbally. The menu had changed in a way that I do not find acceptable. The basic price of the menu was still reasonable but virtually every item that you might have chosen had a supplement attached. The old 80 Franc menu now became 150 Franc menu when you added up the supplements. As if that was not bad enough, when the food arrived it was cold and very badly cooked. What had happened? The old woman who ran the place was still there and the waiters were the same. Later we were told that the *patron* had died in the meantime so although he was not particularly visible in the good old days he had obviously had a considerable influence behind the scenes.

I have not eaten there since but a friend has told me that it has changed again for the better. If it is back to the old formula it will certainly go back on the list.

The following morning we set off to visit Agence Clouzot, the estate agent recommended by our man Singleton in Richmond. We arrived at the small town after a pleasant fifteen minute drive and had no difficulty locating Agence Clouzot. It turned out that Monsieur Clouzot spoke pretty good English so communication did not look as if it was going to be a problem. The reason that I have given him the name Clouzot is because he reminded me a bit of Inspector Clouzot in the Pink Panther films - not so much in looks as in actions, or, should I say, lack of positive action. After a considerable amount of shuffling great wads of papers on his desk and generally looking harassed he eventually managed to find us a list of properties to take away with us and study. We arranged a *rendezvous* for the following day to inspect the properties that appeared to be of interest and bade him *au revoir*.

We drove to the beach that afternoon to study our list of properties. The road to the beach was very pleasant; long avenues of trees and small picturesque villages. It took us just over half an hour and convinced us that we were searching in the right area for a house. Not too near the seaside and not too far away either.

The details of the properties were, of course, in French but we managed to get the gist of what it was all about after frequent references to our French/English dictionary. Many of the words and phrases were new to me and certainly not ones that my French teacher had tried to drum into me at school.

We discovered that *rez-de-chausée* means ground floor and *plain pied* is used to indicate that rooms are on a single level. The number of main rooms are indicated by the number of *pièces*. We were already familiar with the *cuisine, chambre, salon* and *séjour*. We were introduced to the *buanderie*, the laundry room, and the *débarras*, the box room.

Moving outside, a *dependance* is an outbuilding and a *remise* becomes a little more specific as it means a garage or barn. A very important item is to determine whether you are buying a house with a *fosse septique* which is a septic tank or if you will be connected to main drainage indicated by *tout-à-l'égout*.

If you are interested in the appearance of the house itself then *pierre apparente* tells you that it is exposed stone which is generally very attractive. Rough cast rendering, or *crépi*, is used on the exterior of a lot of village houses and this can be quite acceptable if it is in good repair.

Other features to look for are *voûté* and *poutre*. *Voûté* means that the room is vaulted. This is almost always on the *rez-de-chausée* level where the animals used to be kept in days gone by. It is strange to consider that the area the animals occupied is now considered to be the most attractive part of a house. *Poutres* are exposed beams which can also add considerably to the appearance of a room.

Carrelage is floor tiling and many of the village houses have old *terre cuite* tiles on the floor. If these are not broken then they are well worth keeping.

Tuiles romanes is the traditional form of roof tile to be found in the South of France. When these tiles reach the eaves they are formed into a *génoise* which really means that there are several thicknesses of them. Apparently the richer the owner the more tiles he would have in his *génoise*. If a house has a good *génoise* the estate agent will always draw your attention to this feature. If a house has a *génoise* in need of repair a builder will always stare at it for a long time shaking his head and you can visualise the repair bill increasing in leaps and bounds.

As far as we were concerned the most important thing to look for, in the house descriptions, was a terrace, or as a fallback, *possibilité de terrasse*. It would also be nice to be on the *tout-à-l'égout* rather than to rely on a *fosse septique* and *pierre apparente* would be preferable to *crépi*. We were beginning to get the hang of this.

Next morning we were at Agence Clouzot spot on time. We had marked all the properties that interested us and started to go through the list with Monsieur Clouzot. The first property was OK - he would show it to us that morning. Then things went downhill. We would point to a property and he would shake his head and score a pencil through it or he would confer with a very elegant lady who was obviously his assistant. She would shake her head and out would come the pencil.

We had started with a list of about fifteen properties that we wanted to look at plus several others that we wanted further information on. When Monsieur Clouzot was finished we had two properties to look at, both in a small village just ten minutes drive away.

The first house had distinct possibilities. It was situated on a corner, not a right angle corner but a very acute angle corner that gave the house some character. The roof at the front could be chopped off and a very nice little terrace constructed. It was small with a kitchen, bathroom, two bedrooms and a small *cave* but sufficient for our needs and pocket. It also had a separate garden. You get this quite often with village houses and usually the garden is of no use as it is some distance from the house. In this case it was just across the road and very nicely located overlooking a tennis court. It had a built-in barbecue and would serve very nicely until the terrace was built.

The only problem with the house was that it was overfurnished. Chests of drawers were stacked one on top of the other in all the rooms and although some of the furniture was quite attractive, at least half of it would have to go before the house would be habitable. We did ask Monsieur Clouzot if the furniture was included in the price but I got the impression that he did not really know from the non-committal sort of answer he gave.

Taking everything into account it was a nice little house in a good location at an acceptable price. We confirmed our interest. but said we wanted to see some more before we reached a decision.

The next house was bigger but had nothing going for it. There were no attractive features and it was in a hopeless location. It was listed at 350,000 francs and we said that we could not afford that price. Monsieur Clouzot said that we could have it for 180,000 francs. Now after the episode where the list of properties had shrunk from about twenty to two under his pencil we had begun to have our doubts about Monsieur Clouzot. His sudden halving of the price of a house did nothing to allay our growing fears. Perhaps if he had done the same with the first house we would have felt differently.

We said, once again, that we liked the first house but really must look at more than just two properties.

Monsieur Clouzot pondered. He consulted his list and scratched his head. It took a long time but at least there was no elegant assistant there to shake her head.

'What about a *mas?*' he asked.

Now we knew that a *mas* was a farmhouse and although it was far from being a village house we thought that we had better have a look as the price was very attractive.

We drove out into the country and soon came to this very small building. A dog was barking somewhere nearby.

CAN THIS BE A TYPICAL FRENCH ESTATE AGENT?

'It is very small,' Monsieur Clouzot said, as we approached the building.

It became apparent that the barking was coming from the building itself. It was obviously being used as a dog kennel. In retrospect he could have said *mazet*, which is a small barn, instead of *mas* as that would certainly have been a more accurate description.

'A little too small, I think,' we confided in him.

'We will return to the office,' he said.

Back in the office under the ever watchful eye of his assistant he consulted even more papers.

'Ah,' he said, 'a possibility, but it will need a lot of work done on it.'

'Tell us about it,' we encouraged him.

He began to talk and as he talked I could see the elegant lady shaking her head but, bravely, he ventured on with the description.

'*Non*!'

He looked at her then timidly approached her. The exchange in French was too fast for me to follow but when he returned and before he could say anything I said. 'We really would like to have a look at the house.'

He looked at her again then turned back to me and shrugged his shoulders apologetically. His look said everything; it was pointless for me to pursue the matter.

'Would you be interested in a flat in this town?' he asked. 'It is on the top floor and there is the possibility of a terrace.'

I conferred with Barbara and we agreed that it was a nice small town and a flat was worth considering. Things were looking up again but just to make sure I checked with the elegant lady. Yes, all was well.

'Let me get the key,' he said and began shuffling papers and opening drawers and looking in cupboards. He had a consultation with his assistant then returned to us.

'I cannot find the key,' he said, 'but I will show you the flat from the outside.'

We walked with him a short distance and he pointed upwards. The flat was nicely located over some shop premises. We decided that we would like to see the flat so asked him what the next move was.

'Let us meet in my office tomorrow afternoon at two o'clock,' he said, 'and I will have the key.'

We agreed.

We arrived at his office at two o'clock the following day and the office was closed. There was no sign of life anywhere.

Perhaps he will be along in a few minutes we thought and retired to a *café* across the street for a drink. Barbara also wanted to use the toilet.

When she returned from the toilet she looked a bit flustered.

'I did not like that at all,' she said.

The toilet had been clean enough but it had been situated half way up a staircase open to the world. She had been convinced that people were going to appear at any minute going up and down the stairs.

It is, of course, quite a common occurrence in the *Hommes* to be standing and delivering whilst the lady in charge of the toilet is doing a bit of cleaning and polishing next to you. I remember the occasion when I visited Brussels with an American colleague who was not familiar with such quaint customs. When we arrived at the airport we went to the toilet. Now this guy was strictly Mid-West Bible Belt where you would not even use the word toilet within hearing distance of a decent woman. As we went about our business the toilet lady wandered in and began to mop the floor behind us. This was a totally new experience for my companion who zipped up and fled almost before he had started.

French toilets are, to me, a bit like horses. I find them interesting to look at but I am often not at all happy about sitting on them. The most interesting ones are, of course, the old fashioned sort where there is a hole in the floor and two moulded footprints to help you position yourself.

There was a *footprint* toilet in a *café* in Pouilly en Auxois that provided us with a great deal of entertainment. We had gone to the *café* for an *apéritif* before returning to the hotel to dine. It was the height of the season so there were a lot of visitors. A feature of the toilet was that it had an extremely vicious flushing mechanism. I discovered this quite early in the proceedings but as it was a warm evening my shoes soon dried out.

Some people, however, made the mistake of flushing the toilet before they had completely adjusted their clothing. When faced with the prospect of death by drowning in a French toilet or a slight loss of dignity by leaping partly clothed into a crowded *café* they always chose the latter option. It was great fun as we all waited in eager anticipation each time a new arrival paid a visit. I am sure that the *café* owner was in no hurry to have the toilet flush adjusted due to the entertainment it provided his customers.

David once owned a house somewhere in the middle of France where, he said, the people were a bit strange. It was a very isolated region and there was a lot of inbreeding. He said he once found a toilet there with three footprints. I wonder if it was true?

After about half an hour we saw Monsieur Clouzot approaching his office. Well, perhaps half an hour late was not considered excessive in this part of the world. We would just settle the bill for our drinks and then wander over.

Monsieur Clouzot approached his office, drew level with his office, passed his office and disappeared into the distance.

We decided that we had had enough of Monsieur Clouzot.

CHAPTER 5

Alphonse Delivers the Goods

Villegrande has a population of several thousand. Our map told us this. If you buy the large scale maps they give you the populations of all the towns and villages.

A town this size, we decided, must have a few estate agents. As the Singleton connection had drawn a blank we had to try elsewhere or our trip would be a waste of time so we set off to walk round the town and see what we could discover.

Villegrande is a pleasant French provincial town. If it has a unique claim to fame we did not discover it. There are busy crossroads in the centre which, during the tourist season, are under the control of a traffic policeman. The shrill blast of his whistle is heard incessantly and his gesticulations soon manage to bring the traffic to a standstill. His allocation of priority seemed to defy reason and the only hint I got of any semblance of order was that he seemed to give preference to attractive young ladies. It would not surprise me to find out that he is employed by the tourist board. The two main *cafés* are just by the crossroads and all the customers seem to enjoy his antics.

Crossroads in French are *carrefour*. To me Carrefour is a supermarket like Tesco or Sainsbury's. It was at Macon, I think, that I asked the lady at the toll booth for directions to the Ibis Hotel. She told me to turn right at the *carrefour*. I went round the *carrefour* about twenty times looking for a Carrefour.

We found an estate agent by the crossroads. It was called Agence Pons. We had a good look at the cards in the window but they did not really tell us a great deal. Between the rows of cards we could see Monsieur Pons sitting at his desk. He looked fairly normal and as he was alone we decided to have a chat to him.

It was encouraging to see that Monsieur Pons seemed well organised and that Monsieur Clouzot was, perhaps, not typical of French estate agents. Despite the fact that Monsieur Pons spoke no English we managed to communicate reasonably well.

He did not have any properties that met our requirements but he knew a man who did. The man in question was his son, who was also in the business, with an office in a smaller town not too far distant. We will call the smaller town Villemarché because it is big enough to have a market once a week. He gave his son a call and, sure enough, he had a couple of properties on his books that seemed to meet our requirements. He arranged an appointment for us to meet his son the following day. That was it. We felt we had done enough for one day so we retired to the *café* for a leisurely pastis and to enjoy the entertainment provided by the tourist board's traffic policeman.

After our drink we booked out of the hotel as it was now time to seek out David and move in with him for a couple of days.

David lived in a village house in quite a large village about ten kilometres from Villegrande. When we arrived at the house there was nobody at home. This was not surprising as we had not agreed any particular time of arrival. Lunch was the next thing on the agenda so off we went in search of food. This should have been no problem at all in a village of this size but we searched far and wide and could not find a restaurant. In the end we found a small *café* where we managed to get a sandwich.

We tried David's house again. Still no sign of life so this time we set off round the village looking for *A VENDRE* signs. We did not see very many houses for sale and the ones that we did see were not really of any interest. We also had come to the conclusion that this was not really the sort of village that we were looking for. For one thing it did not seem to have a village square. The great thing about the classic French village is that it has a square with a fountain, a war memorial, a *café* and last, but not least, a *pissoir*.

David and Lyn were there when we returned for the second time so we unloaded the car and settled in for a couple of days before we were due to move on to meet Taff and Melanie.

In fact, they should already have arrived at their hotel so David decided that he would invite them to dinner that evening along with another couple they knew who lived nearby called Jeff and Dominique.

Jeff, like most of us hen-pecked males could not definitely commit until he spoke to Dominique, his other half who was still at work. Taff and Melanie had arrived at the hotel but they were out so a message had to be left for them. By eight o'clock there was still no news and it looked as if the four of us were going to have to tackle a mountain of food and a lake of wine all on our own.

Just after eight thirty Jeff and Dominique arrived and within five minutes Taff and Melanie turned up. Suddenly we were eight and the wine began to flow.

David had acquired a forty litre container of a good local red wine, at a staggering cost of about 120 francs. That worked out around three francs a litre so David was not serving up rubbish; we were drinking at the high end of his expenditure range. He fully expected this container to last him for the three weeks that he would be there. We had other ideas. He had a jug that held about two litres and he would go down three flights of stairs to the *cave* to fill the jug. I do not know how many trips he made but it was a lot. He got a great deal of exercise and we all got very merry.

Jeff and Dominique were a very pleasant young couple. David had met Jeff, who is English, in the area where he had bought his first house in France. Jeff had helped him with the work on the house and when David had acquired his new house he asked Jeff, who was between jobs at the time, if he would like to come down south for a couple of weeks to give him a hand. Jeff had met Dominique through some mutual friends and it had been love at first sight. Jeff never went back North. That had been a few years previously. Jeff took whatever jobs he could get in the area and did not seem at all concerned that he was not creating a serious long term career for himself. He appeared to be entirely contented with his lot. He was such a relaxed, agreeable sort of fellow that everyone immediately took to him.

'I hate him', I whispered to Taff.

'Me too', He said. 'He has really got it made down here.'

It was only jealousy, of course, and the knowledge that in a couple of weeks we would have to return to the hard graft, the grey skies, the incessant rain.

We were not in good shape the following morning but we decided that we had to persevere with the search for a house so off we went to Villemarché.

Alphonse Pons, son of Monsieur Pons of Villegrande, turned out to be a clean cut young man who spoke French very slowly, clearly and precisely. This is very unusual in a Frenchman but perhaps he had some special training. Generally, French people fire words at you at machine gun speed. When you ask them to repeat them more slowly, instead of doing so, they completely rephrase the whole thing and belt it out at the same rate.

It was a pleasure to listen to Alphonse Pons.

He had two houses that he could show us that day. The first was in a village that we had driven through. We had not put a circle round the village on the map which meant that our first impressions of the place had not been all that good. Alphonse told us that the house needed a lot of renovation but was very cheap.

The second house was in a village that we had not heard of but it did have quite an impressive name. I shall call it St. Crispin de la Forêt. This house was in *très bon état*, had a terrace of sorts and was a bit more expensive.

I certainly liked the names of the villages particulary St. Crispin de la Forêt - a touch of class there.

The first house was not bad. It would need new plumbing and rewiring but it had some attractive features, not least of which was a little garden in the back. The garden seemed to get a good deal of sunshine, unlike a lot of little back gardens in France where the sun never seems to shine. It also had a well in the garden which was a nice touch. On the downside, even though there was a terrace it did not belong to the house, despite the fact that it was outside one of the bedroom windows. There was barbed wire across the window. Was this to deter people from using the terrace or was it to stop terrace users entering the bedroom? Definitely a minus point but the price was good. Only 140,000 francs.

'*C'est un très bon prix,*' said Alphonse.

I made one of the French signs that I had learned that saved me from relying upon my limited French. I turned down my lips at the corners and a waggled my hands which I felt indicated that I was not fantastically impressed but was not absolutely rejecting the possibility. The house had potential but I was not sure about the village. It was quite a large village so you had the advantages of local shops but there did not really seem to be any centre to it and it was on a main road.

St. Crispin de la Forêt was about two kilometres off the main road. We saw the sign for St. Crispin just by the *Cave Cooperative*. A couple of hundred yards further on we came to the village square or rather two village squares joined together. The first was called the Place des Jeux de Ballons and the second the Place de la République. There was a fountain. There was a war memorial. There was a *café*. There was an *alimentation*. There was a *tabac*. And there was a *pissoir*. It was a proper village square.

We were even more pleased to discover that the house in question actually fronted on to the square at the corner of the Place de la République and Rue Renoir.

Our first impression was that the house was indeed in *très bon état* because it was nicely *crépied*. I would have preferred *pierre apparente* but it was certainly not a show stopper.

The ground floor consisted of a kitchen, a bathroom and a small *cave*. All of this in about 30 square metres. There was a nice big fireplace in the kitchen that could take logs about a metre long and from the various accoutrements lying around it was obvious that the previous occupants had been keen on the *feu de bois* style of cooking.

There was a decent kitchen sink and space next to it for a fridge. In the cave there was a large immersion heater, plumbing for a washing machine and a fair amount of storage space.

The bathroom was without a bidet, presumably because there was no room for one, but otherwise fully equipped. No work required there.

The whole of the ground floor, with the exception of the cave, was tiled in these very expensive looking octagonal floor tiles, the designer sort where every tenth tile or so has a little signature on it. The wallpaper was dreadful but there was not a great deal of it as the whole of the ground floor was vaulted. The first floor was devoted entirely to the salon. Same floor tiles and another large fireplace, this time in white

stone and obviously not used. The wallpaper was dreadful. A very nice feature of the salon was that the old stone *font*, or sink, had been preserved with a sort of alcove and we immediately saw the potential for some glass shelves across the alcove for the glasses and the bottles could go in the font.

We proceeded upstairs again and we were shown two small bedrooms leading off the landing. The whole of the top floor had fitted carpet which was a nice neutral colour and in good condition. The wallpaper was dreadful.

'*Et maintenant la terrasse*,' announced Alphonse, standing on the landing and flourishing a pole with a hook on the end.

He pulled down a very substantial metal loft ladder which led up to a trap-door. We all clambered up and on to the flat concrete roof of the house. We were as high as any of the other houses in the village so we had a very good view in all directions. We could also look down into the square and see what was going on. Or rather we could have looked down if there had been something to stop us falling off the edge. On two sides there were walls adjoining the roofs of other houses but the remaining two sides needed something done before one could consider using the roof as a terrace.

'*C'est nécessaire à fabriquer un mur*,' confided Alphonse just in case we had not noticed the slight discrepancy. He said that there would be no problem getting permission.

We liked the house and we liked the village but there was still the price.

'*Deux cent mille francs*,' said Alphonse, '*mais c'est en très bon état et prêt pour occuper sans travail*.' He confirmed that the house had been rewired recently and really needed nothing major doing to it. The people selling it were French. They had come down from Lyon a couple of years ago because of the husband's job but there had been some problem with his health so they were going back to Lyon. They had already reduced the price twice and Alphonse did not think that they would go below 200,000 francs. I said that it seemed a fair price and that we were interested but before we made up our mind did he have any more houses to show us.

He had one more that he would show us the next day so we made an appointment for ten the following morning.

As soon as he dropped us in Villemarché we got into our car and drove back to St. Crispin de la Forêt to have a closer look at the village.

One of the things that Barbara was very keen on was that our village should have its own *boulangerie* as we did not want to have to get in the car to get the bread in the morning.

We had not seen a *boulangerie* in the village so we kept our eyes open as we wandered around. We went into the *alimentation* but they did not seem to sell bread.

This was serious. Everything else seemed to be perfect. Now I know that I am not an observant person but nothing escapes Barbara. We were just about to admit defeat when she saw the small sign above the *pissoir*. It pointed up a narrow street and said *BUCHERIE, BOULANGERIE*.

The reason why Barbara had not seen it before was because she always averts her eyes when passing French *pissoirs* for obvious reasons. We followed the sign and found the shops in a little square in the middle of the village.

We had lunch in Villemarché and talked ourselves into buying the house. We could put a wall round the terrace and we could replace the loft ladder with a spiral staircase. There was enough to keep me occupied for quite a while. There was also another reason. Each time that we had bought a house in England it had been the second house that we looked at. So why not the same in France?

We went back to see Alphonse and told him that we would take the house. He was pleased but were we sure that we did not want to see the other house tomorrow? Yes, we were sure, but we would like to have a closer inspection of the house in St. Crispin.

He said that he would have the paperwork ready for me to sign tomorrow morning and in the meantime why not take the key and examine the house at our leisure.

Another reason for buying the house was the name of the village. St. Crispin de la Forêt sounded pretty impressive. We had no idea who St. Crispin was but we did get a bit of history on him, from an old book, a couple of years later.

Crispin (which, of course, is not his real name because I have changed it to protect the village from too many prying eyes) was born in the *Gaulle Narbonnaise* in the second or third century A.D. He was converted to catholicism as a young man and was so taken with his new found faith that he decided to shut himself away from the world and devote himself to prayer.

He chose a section of thick forest, which is today occupied by the village of St. Crispin de la Forêt, as the location of his first hermitage. Although the forest was very thick it was not completely uninhabited. Crispin's prayers kept being interrupted by strange people passing through his stretch of woods. Not surprisingly, the people he discovered in the forest were heathens so Crispin took up the task of converting them with great enthusiasm. As the heathens were, no doubt, passionately engaged in the French pastime of *la chasse* it is quite surprising that Crispin's efforts in the field of religious instruction did not result in him becoming the quarry.

There is no record of how long he remained in this place but at some stage he moved on to a second hermitage in a desolate spot on the rock strewn slopes approaching the *Massif Central*.

Perhaps Crispin moved to this unappealing, rocky terrain with its river gorges just for change of scenery or perhaps he wanted even more isolation.

He settled at the foot of a rock face and it was there that he created for himself his second claim to fame. He marked the rock in such a way that he could tell the time by the shadows cast on it by the sun. He had created a sundial and in this part of the world there are many sundials that are called *Roc de Crispin*.

Our old book informs us that, out of the large number of localities that have taken Saint-Crispin as their patron, not a single one has adopted both applications of his name. Nowhere is the village called Saint-Crispin and a sundial in the village called *Roc de Crispin*. Make of that what you will.

The next we hear of Crispin is that he has given up the solitary life and gone off and joined the *Gallo-Romaine* army. Did this mean that he was questioning his beliefs? Certainly not. His faith was as strong as ever and he spent all his time teaching Christianity and converting the heathens to the true faith. I suppose he just looked around to see where he could find the densest population of heathens and opted for the army.

It was while he was garrisoned in the town of Nîmes that he became a martyr and was elevated to Sainthood. He had gone for a stroll outside the walls of the city when he came upon a group who were in the process of offering sacrifices to false gods. He pointed out to them, in a very polite fashion, the error of their ways and suggested that they desist immediately from such practices. They beat him up. This did not deter Crispin who continued to try to convert them. In the end they cut off his head. This did act as a fairly effective deterrent but the die had been cast and he had now established himself as a martyr.

CHAPTER 6

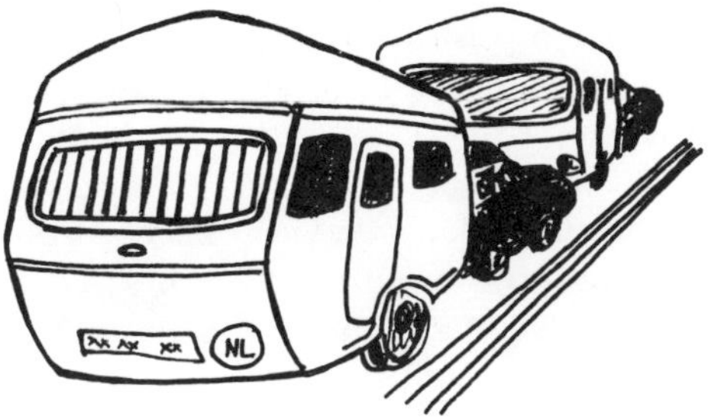

No Deposit Necessary

I needed an expert opinion on the house in St. Crispin de la Forêt so I took David along to have a look at it.

David's hobby is buying and selling houses although he will not admit to it. He always claims that the houses he buys are going to be permanent residences for the rest of his natural life.

The houses he buys are usually in a very good state of repair but alterations are always necessary to meet his particular requirements. Within days he will have architects and builders crawling all over developing plans and estimates for major reconstruction work. The end result is always very attractive but he has sweated blood to achieve it. It is not unusual for him to fall out with his builder at some stage of the proceedings.

When a house is completed to David's satisfaction he will hold a house-warming party. This is a sure sign that the house will be on the market within weeks.

David gave the house the thumbs up so I felt comfortable that I was doing the right thing. *Maison Simpson* would soon become a reality.

David also accompanied me when I went to see Alphonse Pons to make sure that I was not committing myself to more than I had bargained for.

It was all very simple and straightforward really. Alphonse asked me to sign a bit of paper called a *Compromis de Vente* which committed me to ten per cent of the purchase price if I did not go through with the deal.

I then pulled my wad of 500 franc notes out of my pocket and offered him 20,000 francs as a deposit.

'*C'est pas nécessaire*' he said. I pressed him, as I wanted to get rid of all this cash, but he just smiled and shook his head. So much for your always having to pay a deposit.

Alphonse said that completion would be in about six weeks time which would be around the middle of October. The lawyer who does the conveyancing is a called a *Notaire* and he recommended that we used *Maître* Fabre who had an office across the street. Apparently the buyer has the choice of *Notaire* and as I had no other contenders I accepted the recommendation.

I had, to all intents and purposes, bought a house and, as a by-product, arranged another little holiday in the South of France for October. I was already beginning to warm to the idea of being a French property owner as that would be my third holiday in France that year.

It was now time to take our leave of David and book into the hotel where Taff was staying. The hotel, as we expected, was situated in a very peaceful location, up in the hills, a few kilometres from the nearest main road.

The hotel was run by a very attractive young lady who claimed to be Dutch. However, I was not entirely convinced of her nationalistic claims for two main reasons. Firstly, she did not speak English, and all the Dutch people I had ever met spoke excellent English, more often than not, superior to my own. Secondly, and this is the clincher, she did not appear to own a caravan. Now, as we all know, every Dutch person owns at least one caravan and during the summer months Holland is empty. They are to be found on every Route Nationale in France, travelling in convoy, to avoid any possibility of a faster moving vehicle overtaking them. However, in retrospect, she probably did own a caravan and, as she was not using it, had lent it to someone else so that its full disruptive potential could be exploited.

We found Taff and Melanie relaxing by the swimming pool. Taff told us that they had brought their folding cycles in the back of the car and the previous day they had done a tour of several villages. They had already rejected some villages as this would save time at the estate agents.

They had, in fact, toured a lot more villages than they had intended to because of Melanie's infatuation with a garage mechanic.

Taff had just taken possession of a new company car, a Renault 25, and it was due for a 1000 mile service.

'Why not have it done in France?', he thought, so he telephoned the local Renault garage.

They drove up to the garage in Villegrande early the next morning and parked in the road outside. Taff unloaded the bicycles from the back of the car and began to assemble them whilst Melanie, who spoke good French, went off to sort out the details. She returned shortly, slightly flustered, with a dreamy look in the eyes, and confided in Taff that the mechanic was the absolute epitome of her ideal sexy Frenchman. He was tall and slim with dark brooding eyes and dark curly hair and when he smiled, well . . .

'Did Jean Paul Belmondo say when the car would be ready?' asked Taff, who was already wondering about the wisdom of the cycle trip as the sun was getting hotter by the minute.

'At noon,' Melanie replied.

'Good, so we can pick it up and then go for a nice lunch.'

They cycled and cycled through village after village building up their dossier and when they eventually returned to Villegrande at noon they were pretty exhausted.

Taff thought it wise to accompany Melanie this time when she went to look for the mechanic in case they decided to run off together in his new car. They found him sitting with his feet up on the desk enjoying a Gauloise.

'*Ah bon*,' said Melanie, giving him a big smile. '*Le révision est terminée?*'

'*Non*,' he replied without a smile. '*Je n'ai pas commencé le révision*.'

'*Mais pourquoi, non?*' Now Melanie was not smiling. '*Vous m'avez dit que la voiture serait prête à midi*.'

Taff with his limited French was having no difficulty following this exchange.

'*Oui Madame, et la voiture serait prête si vous m'aviez donné la clef*.'

Melanie gulped and felt in her pocket. The car key was indeed there. She humbly proffered the key and they left with the assurance that the car would be ready by four o'clock. Plenty of time for lunch and a few more villages.

David had heard very good reports of a restaurant in the area run by an Englishman so we decided to give it a try. It is called the Mimosa and it is situated in a small, picturesque village called St. Guiraud.

When we arrived we received a very warm welcome from David Pugh and his wife Bridget and as we were reasonably early they gave us a tour of the property. It is a delightful old house with a courtyard and it has all been carefully restored. There is a wonderful *cave* containing enormous oak wine casks with a swimming pool that has been built half in the *cave* and half in the courtyard. There is a large indoor dining room with about eight tables and four tables on the terrace overlooking the courtyard. It really is a marvellous setting for a restaurant.

As it was a warm evening we sat on the terrace and sipped our *apéritifs*. There was a choice of two *apéritifs maison*. The first was called a *Mimosa* and consisted of a local dry *vin mousseux* with a spot of *crème de framboise* and a couple of frozen raspberries added. It looked and tasted very pleasant. The second *apéritif*, which became my favourite, was named *Folle Blanche*. My simple, literal, translation of this is *White Madness* but I am sure that David Pugh has either a better translation or a good explanation for mine. It is a mixture of a local white wine called *Picpoul de Pinet*, a little *muscat* and a touch of *Noilly Prat*, served very chilled with a sliver of lime peel.

We were given an *à la carte* menu each which really was quite formidable and when he came back and told us that he also did a *menu de dégustation* at 150 francs we were all ears. He described the courses in loving detail and we decided that this was for us. If the food was half as good as the way he described it we were in for a very satisfying meal. As it turned out the food was excellent and although David deserves credit for his descriptive eloquence the true genius is Bridget who prepares all the wonderful food. Everything, of course, is home made and David Pugh even smokes his own salmon.

There is an extensive wine list ranging from the very best of the local wines to very expensive wines. We always drink the local wines, partly for economic reasons, but mainly because we like them and you can rely on David Pugh to find the best that are to be had locally. He will

NO DEPOSIT NECESSARY

tell you whether to go for the *Clairette* or the *Picpoul de Pinet* for your white and will almost certainly have a good *Faugères* to recommend for the red.

The Mimosa has been very well received by the local French population and, even in the tourist season, the majority of the customers are French. This is probably just as well from the point of view of profit as they tend to buy the expensive wines. David Pugh certainly knows his wines and you can see that the French are impressed. They hold long conversations with him, their noses inserted in their glasses and I will swear that at times they never actually get round to drinking the wine.

David Pugh also waxes eloquent on the subject of cheese. He will produce an enormous cheese board and proceed to describe each item in great detail. I have not actually put him to the test but I am sure that he could give you the individual names of the goats that contributed to the making of his selection of *chèvres*.

David Pugh told us that he had been an orchestral violinist and Bridget a member of the Royal Ballet until a couple of years before when they had decided to pack it all in, move to France, and open up a restaurant. He said that it had been tough but things were looking up a bit and he had actually had a celebrity visit his restaurant a few weeks ago. It had been one of the female stars from an American soap opera called Dynasty.

'Have you heard of the show,' he asked.

'Yes', I said. 'It is very popular at home. Terry Wogan refers to it as Dysentery.'

'Who is Terry Wogan?' David Pugh enquired.

To discover an Englishman who had never heard of Terry Wogan was a most refreshing experience. I cannot remember what my response was but I am sure that it was totally inadequate in terms of describing the charm, charisma and searing wit of the megastar himself.

'She was sitting at one of the tables on the terrace enjoying her meal,' David Pugh continued, 'when a dog decided to go into the swimming pool and could not get out. It was obviously in great distress so she rushed over and pulled it out.'

'I wish I had got a photograph of her pulling the dog out,' he said. 'I could have got it into the national press with the caption '*SOAP STAR SAVES DOG FROM DROWNING AT EXCLUSIVE RESTAURANT.*'

'Yes, it is a pity,' I agreed, 'but you would probably have found that a more appropriate caption, bearing in mind the characters of Dynasty, would have been '*SOAP STAR TRIES TO DROWN DOG AT EXCLUSIVE RESTAURANT*.'

Taff and Melanie found a house they liked in one of their approved villages a few days later. It was a big house and it needed a lot of work done on it. They thought about it for a while then decided to go ahead.

They would get an architect to do the plans for the renovation and he would hire the builder, the plumber and the electrician. It would not be cheap but in the end they would have a very desirable residence. In my case I had spent all the money I could afford on my house. Any additional work that had to be done would have to be done by me, ably assisted, of course, by my willing helpmate, Barbara.

CHAPTER 7

Of Customs and Careers

When I visited my UK bank to borrow the money to pay for the house I found them to be a model of efficiency. I suspect that it was something to do with the branch manager achieving his monthly quota of mortgage loans. He saw me personally, which was unusual, and certainly seemed to be very anxious to lend me the money. I had not noticed the same level of interest when I wanted to open an overseas bank account but then I doubt that such an item would figure very prominently in the bank manager's monthly measurement system.

He was a very dynamic young man with a touch of the wheeler dealer about him. Not at all the sort of chap I was expecting but then it was probably fifteen years since I had last seen a bank manager in the flesh. I was used to the old school of bank manager. This chap actually smiled and cracked jokes. As my current mortgage was small and did not even reach the maximum for tax allowances he suggested that I claim tax relief on part of the amount I was borrowing for the overseas property.

'But surely that is not allowed?' I questioned him.

He ignored the question.

'If they do ask you to produce receipts I am sure you can come up with some,' he continued.

Even though I had no intention of misleading the Inland Revenue in such a way, I gave him the impression that I would follow his advice.

Such initiative was, in my experience very unusual in your run-of-the-mill bank manager and I did not want to stifle his enthusiasm.

In a few weeks time we would be the owners of a small village house in France and although it was in '*très bon état*' and ready for occupation it was devoid of even the barest essentials in the furnishing line. Now was the time to start collecting.

We spread the word around our relations that anything, however dilapidated, would be welcome. There was an initial reluctance to offer us items that they considered to be a bit too grotty but once they realised how desperate we were the offers flowed in.

By the time we were ready to leave for France we had accumulated a substantial load. It never ceases to amaze me how much can be packed into the family car.

There was no question of hiring a proper removal firm to do the job. The interest payments on my bank loan would take up all my spare cash so now we had to get the house into a habitable condition with the minimum of financial outlay.

It was for this reason that I had arranged my trip to France around a business trip to our European HQ in Paris where I had to do a presentation to our senior European HQ management. This meant that the ferry was paid for both ways and the tolls as far as Paris. Petrol, which is much more expensive in France, was not a concern as the company paid for all my petrol, even when on holiday abroad. This, I must say, was quite a significant factor in our decision to buy a house in the South of France.

The car was packed to the gunwales and I had to travel in my business suit as there was nowhere it could be stowed without being crushed.

We took the Portsmouth–Le Havre route even though we had been unable to book a cabin. As soon as we were on board we rushed along to see if there were any cancellations but no such luck.

It was my first experience of club class reclining seats and I hope it will be my last. The advantage of a cabin is that the likelihood of people passing through it while you are trying to sleep is pretty small. In the club lounge there seemed to be an endless stream of people going in all directions. Just as it appeared to be quietening down I heard a familiar sound. It was the patter of little feet on the deck above. Why is it that on boats there always seem to be children running around on the deck above even in the middle of the night?

I think I slept for a whole five minutes.

As I was going to the office I had to have a shave. The only place to do this was the Gents toilet. This was another first for me. I had always considered the sort of people you see shaving in public toilets to be rather shifty and I felt very uncomfortable as I stood there stripped to the waist attending to my ablutions.

The business meeting was due to start at 10 a.m. and I was first on the agenda. My plan was that I would give my presentation to the assembled company, try to avoid any questions, do a quick change into something more comfortable in the executive toilets and we would be on our way. My ETA at the office was 9.30 a.m. so I could afford half an hour's delay.

I had been to France many times by ferry and I had never been stopped by the French Customs. In general, the *Douane Française* do not seem to care who enters France or what they bring in with them. It never occurred to me that I would be stopped on this occasion and I had certainly not built in any contingency factor to allow for it.

Perhaps the *Grand Patron de Douane* was visiting Le Havre that day and they were putting on a show for him. Whatever the reason, as I approached the customs office, instead of the usual cursory glance and wave on, I was confronted with a customs officer barring my way. He gave me a very stern look and indicated that I should pull over into a small bay.

He walked round the car twice then asked us to get out. He did not seem at all deterred by the amount of goods and chattels that we had in the car. The car was a hatchback and the sensible thing would have been for him to ask me to open the back door. He asked me to open one of the side doors. I did consider trying to explain to him that things would fall out if I opened the door but after one look at his face I decided to open the door. Things fell out on to the ground but luckily nothing breakable.

The customs officer considered the things on the ground then picked up a six pack of Andrex toilet rolls. He gave me a disdainful look and handed me the package. Had he given me the opportunity I would have vigorously defended Andrex as being vastly superior to any brand

POLI
ARRET
8EFP
GB

of French toilet paper that we had come across. Would he find the tins of baked beans and the large jar of Branston pickle I wondered and, if he did, would he appreciate that there was no French equivalent.

As he could see that nothing further was going to fall out of the side door he asked me to open the back door.

A large part of the back of the car was occupied by a fridge. It was an old fridge as was easily determined by the rust marks on the base. As we had more to take down than we had space for in the car we had made absolute maximum use of the space available. This included packing things inside the fridge. If he wanted to open up the fridge to see what was inside then we were in for a long delay as just about everything in the back of the car would have to be unloaded to achieve this.

I breathed a sigh of relief when I saw that he had turned his attention to my briefcase. I suppose this was because it looked a bit out of place amongst the toilet rolls and baked beans. When he opened it he seemed to be particularly interested in the transparencies that I had prepared for my presentation. He scrutinised each one in great detail and eventually I began to wonder if he was perhaps a part-time industrial espionage agent.

As time went on it became obvious that he was not looking for anything. This was simply a time-wasting exercise and he was not making the slightest effort to conceal the fact. Had we upset the French recently? Perhaps there was a problem over imported lamb or, more likely, we had beaten one of their football teams. Whatever the reason, we were suffering because of it.

Half an hour later we were on the road again. I just had time to make my meeting in Paris if I put my foot down and there were no more delays.

We had just passed through the dock gates and were approaching the first set of traffic lights in Le Havre, when what I took to be a *gendarme* leapt out into the road and waved me into a lay by. He was, in fact, a customs officer and he wanted to search our car. I could not believe this.

This time he showed no interest at all in the back of the car. He pointed at the blue bag which rested on the floor by Barbara's feet. We always take the blue bag with us on holiday. It has a pocket for passports, money, tickets, etc. and we stuff the main compartment with books, cameras, sunglasses and of course Barbara's handbag which he extracted and opened. He looked inside and after rummaging around for a while pulled out her wallet. Was this a hint that a small bribe would be appreciated to speed us on our way? I decided not. He ignored the money in the wallet but carefully scrutinized every scrap of paper. Visiting cards were examined back and front, sometimes more than once. I was somewhat put out that Barbara's scraps of paper were getting even more attention than my carefully prepared transparencies had received.

Once again it was being made very clear to us that this was not a serious attempt to find hidden contraband but a deliberate attempt to delay us.

I never did find out the reason for the exercise but it now looked doubtful that I would make the meeting on time.

It was as I reached the outskirts of Paris that I thought the strain had been too much for me because I was overtaken by a dog on a motor bike. I was quite relieved when Barbara indicated that she was also witnessing this unusual sight. The dog, which looked like a golden retriever, was not actually driving the motor bike. It was sitting on the pillion, which had been slightly extended, and would lean from side to side as the driver went round bends. The thing which really caught your attention was the fact that the dog was wearing a crash helmet. I would like to have secured some photographic evidence of this unusual sight but by the time the film had been loaded into the camera they had gone.

I was, indeed, late for the meeting which did cause me a little concern. As I have already indicated, I have never been particularly ambitious in terms of furthering my career. On the other hand I did not want to highlight my shortcomings to senior management as my record was not absolutely unblemished and I quite liked my current job.

The personal assistant to the Director General came out to see me. He did not seem too perturbed. He said he had rescheduled my presentation for the afternoon. No early start southwards for me but at least my black mark tally had not been increased.

When the time eventually came for me to do my bit I presented our proposals in a highly professional manner and the UK director for my function nodded his approval. As I was about to exit stage left the Director General himself spoke to me. A great moment indeed.

'Which other functions have reviewed these proposals?' he asked.

Without thinking I replied, 'Pricing, Legal and the French Customs'.

It would have been fine if he had asked me to explain but he just gave me a strange look and indicated that I could leave.

We were soon to meet again. I took my overnight bag to the toilets to make the change from business executive to casual holiday goer. All would have been well if I had chosen one of the disabled toilets which has a large lockable cubicle. I had not and I had also decided that a complete change of clothes in the small confines of the normal cubicle was not on.

I was standing in the middle of the toilet trying to pull my tracksuit trousers over my trainers when the Director General and one of his colleagues walked in. Once again all I got were strange looks and no opportunity to explain.

All in all I decided that I had not furthered my career by leaps and bounds in the previous few hours.

CHAPTER 8

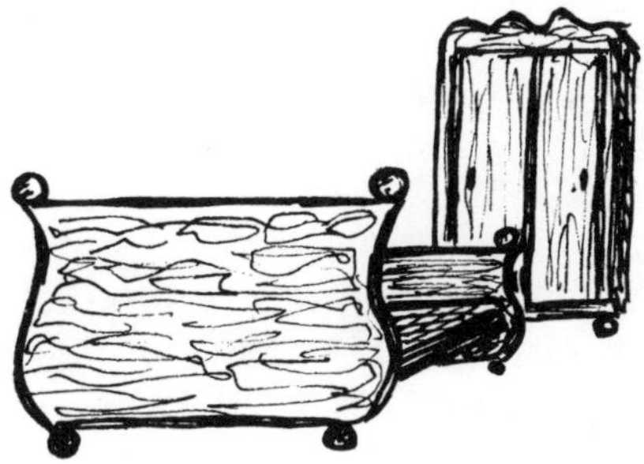

Tin Beds and Bicycles

As I drove south my mind did not dwell upon my lacklustre performance with senior management. I was much more concerned with what awaited me in Villemarché.

'I am not sure about this,' I said.

'About what?' Barbara yawned.

'About entering into a transaction involving a substantial sum of money when I will not understand a word of what is being said.'

'Do you mean that you do not trust young Alphonse?' she asked.

'He seems pretty straight,' I conceded, 'But, after all, he is an estate agent.'

'Yes, I see what you mean.'

We drove on in a worried silence.

Alphonse Pons was waiting for us, in his office, with Monsieur and Madame Bonnet. They were the people who were about to sell us a house.

His full name was Pierre Michel Bonnet and he was a welder by profession. He was born on the 23rd of September 1935 at Montargis in the Loiret.

She had been born Josette Zuchelli in Piedimulera, Italy on the 28th of March 1924. Despite the difference in their ages they had been married at the Mairie in Saint-Just-en-Chevalet, Loire, on the 24th February 1962.

They had bought the house in St. Crispin de la Forêt from Mademoiselle Antoinette Francoise Perrier, shopkeeper, who was born in Plombieres-les-Bains, Vosges, on the 8th August 1932, for the sum of 85,000 francs.

Of course I did not know all of this at the time but when I eventually got the deeds to the house they provided me with all this information - and more.

Monsieur Bonnet looked a very jolly sort of fellow as he sat there puffing away at his Gauloise. France seems to be the last true bastion of the smoker. In the UK, a few years ago, it was not uncommon to see people smoking between courses in restaurants. In France, today, you will frequently see diners taking puffs between forkfuls. These are the same people who wax eloquent over the delicate taste of a dish or stick their nose in a glass of wine for up to ten minutes savouring the bouquet. And they do not seem to be at all worried about the harmful effects to their health. Perhaps they feel that their liver will give out long before their lungs so there is no real risk.

Alphonse led us across the road to the office of the *Notaire*, *Maître* Fabre. We were shown into a fairly sombre, empty office by a tiny little lady dressed in black who, one assumed, was his secretary. It was all very Dickensian. Before *Maître* Fabre appeared I had time to read the various certificates on the wall which told me that the present *Maître* Fabre was the current incumbent of a position that had been occupied by a long line of Fabres who had been *Notaires* in Villemarché.

Maître Fabre turned out to be anything but Dickensian and we settled down to the business in hand after brief introductions.

The process is really very simple but takes a bit of time because the *Notaire* has to read the whole document to the assembled company. From time to time, *Maître* Fabre would fix his gaze upon me and stress a point. He was obviously not satisfied with my facial expressions because he would then turn to Alphonse Pons and seek his help. Alphonse would then explain things to me in his nice simple, estate agent manner. I still did not comprehend most of it but I would feign understanding just so that we would not be there all day.

At the end I handed over a cheque to the *Notaire* and he gave me the keys. I was happy. The Bonnets were happy. Alphonse was happy. *Maître* Fabre was happy. It was difficult to tell with the little old lady in black, as she showed us out, but she was probably happy in her own way.

The Bonnets returned with us to Alphonse Pons' office. They had something to tell us.

'*Il y a quelques choses qui restent dans la maison*' Monsieur Bonnet said. '*Un lit et une garde-robe. Nous n'en avens pas besoin. Si vous les voulez - pas de probleme. Autremont les offrez aux villagers.*'

Now it so happened that a bed and a wardrobe would be very useful but it was not that simple. We were, to them, rich foreigners buying a holiday home and the Bonnets were in a totally different situation. They were moving because he had to give up his job due to ill health. I said thank you very much but we must pay you for these things. They laughed and said, '*Non, c'est un cadeau.*'

I protested but they were adamant. Perhaps they were happy with the price that they had got for the house. I hope so.

I had the keys and I was ready to rush off to view our new acquisition but Alphonse had other ideas.

'It is the law,' he said, 'that you take out fire insurance on your property.'

He then explained that he was an agent for one the major French insurance companies. Well, why not? He had steered us right so far.

Alphonse filled in the form for me to sign. I glanced at it as I did not expect to understand too much but I did notice that he had put the age of the property down as 700 years old.

'*Sept cent ans?*' I questioned him. '*C'est vrai?*'

He confirmed the figure. Apparently all the houses on the inner side of the square were around that period. Should I have had a survey carried out after all? It is apparently very unusual to have a village house in France surveyed. The general feeling seems to be that it is unlikely to fall down because it has already stood for a few hundred years.

I signed up for the insurance and paid the premium which was not too expensive. We did discuss the possibility of my insuring the contents as well as the building. In the end I declined to do so for the simple reason that it would have been extremely embarrassing to admit to the minuscule value of the contents that we had amassed to date.

'Anything else?' I asked Alphonse.

He told me that I should visit the *Mairie* at St. Crispin and give them certain details so that the local taxes could be sorted out.

EDIT AGRIC

That was it. We shook hands and off we went to take a closer look at our first second home.

As we drew up opposite our house we noticed the blind man. He was sitting on a chair in front of the Crédit Agricole. We knew he was blind because he had a white stick and was wearing dark glasses.

Our house was across the square from the Crédit Agricole but it was difficult to park outside our house as we would be blocking the road so we parked in the middle of the square. As we alighted from the car I noticed that the blind man had got up and was tapping his way towards us.

I was concerned that he would walk into the car so I waited till he drew near. It turned out that he did not like where we had parked the car. He indicated with waves of his stick that we should put the car a bit further to the left. I duly obliged. I found it incredible how his highly developed sense of hearing could allow him to pinpoint the exact location of our car.

He nodded acceptance of our new parking spot and tapped his way back to his seat. Not a word had been spoken. Could he have told from the sound of our car engine that we were not French? This seemed a pretty good theory until I remembered that I was, in fact, driving a French car.

We stood and admired the house from the outside for a while before we wandered over and unlocked the door.

The first thing we discovered was that the small *cave* contained a bicycle. It was a ladies bicycle, fairly new and in a very good state of repair. It would have been very handy to have a bicycle but it took up too much room in the *cave* so we would have to get rid of it.

We had only been in the house a few minutes when there was a knock at the door. A very serious looking middle aged woman stood there. She introduced herself as Madame Garcia. She said that the Bonnets had borrowed her gas cooker some time ago and now she wanted it back. She indicated the object in question which was a small camping model in a pretty dilapidated state. We were pleased to let her claim her property.

I thought that I should attempt to make some form of conversation so I asked her if she had happened to lend the Bonnets a bicycle as well. Her eyes lit up.

'*Le vélo reste ici?*' she shouted as she shouldered her way past me to the *cave*.

She explained that the bicycle belonged to the Bonnet's daughter. She had her telephone number and would phone her forthwith. What a considerate woman, I thought, worrying about the girl losing her bicycle.

She rushed off and returned almost immediately.

All was well. The daughter did not want the bicycle and had said that Madame Garcia, as a very good friend of the family, could have it.

Had there been time for phone call? I did not really think so, but I decided that it would not be prudent to suggest to Madame Garcia that I doubted her integrity. She seemed a fairly formidable personality, the sort who would make sure that the whole village knew what a distrustful lot the new *Anglais* were. I indicated that she should take the bicycle and said we were most grateful because we needed the space. As I watched Madame Garcia wheeling away her booty I thought that she would not be difficult to find if the Bonnets did return for the bike.

Upstairs we found the bed and the wardrobe. Both were ideal. We had somewhere to hang our clothes and as soon as we bought a mattress we had somewhere to sleep.

It was a tin bed. The headboard and footboard were made of metal painted to look like wood. They were joined together by heavy iron bars and a frame with a sort of thick wire mesh was placed on top.

The net result was very heavy but incredibly comfortable. Eventually we had to get rid of the headboard and footboard. I had not realised it before but I have a habit of putting my hand behind my head in the middle of the night. I do it quite forcibly at times and the resultant noise as my hand hit the metal was quite sufficient to awaken even a heavy sleeper. The sound seemed to go on for some time. I think the bed acted like a giant tuning fork. Barbara was not amused after being awakened a few times. First of all I stopped wearing my watch in bed which improved matters a bit but not nearly enough.

I made a wooden frame and put the bedspring on it. I was left with a headboard, a footboard and two lengths of heavy angle iron that joined them together. I could think of no alternative use for the headboard and footboard so off they went to the local dump. I kept the lengths of angle iron as I felt sure that I would fine a use for them. In the end I found several uses. In fact the last piece has just been used up. Not a bit was wasted.

We decided that it was time to unload the car. We drove it a bit closer to the house. The blind man was still there and I wondered if he was going to object to the new parking spot. All was well until we actually started unloading the car. He got up and this time he took his seat with him. He placed the seat in a position where, had he not been blind, he could have observed the total contents of the car as they were being unloaded.

I was beginning to become a bit suspicious of the blind man.

CHAPTER 9

The Mattress, the Mairie and the Music

We were now residents of 8, Rue Renoir, Saint Crispin de la Forêt.

The most important item, the refrigerator, was installed and purring away. Already the wine and beer were reaching an acceptable level of coolness. There was even a little space left for solids when we got round to doing some serious shopping.

A mattress of sorts had been purchased. We had tried a shop on the edge of Villemarché first of all. They had a large area out front devoted to all sorts of stone ornamentation ranging from little cherubs to full blown fountains bedecked with angels standing ten foot tall. We thought the place was closed but when we tried the door it opened and we stepped into a large showroom filled with expensive looking furniture. There was no sign of life. We tried upstairs and discovered the bedroom furniture. Still no sign of life. The beds also looked very expensive and when we found one with a price tag on it our assumption was proved correct. We thought that they might sell mattresses separately but despite our cries of *Allo* we could not raise any response.

We would have to try elsewhere. There had been some big furniture stores on the outskirts of Montpellier so we set off in that direction.

The first one we came to had a more reasonably priced set of beds than the Villemarché shop but they did not sell mattresses separately. The only bed they had within our price range was a folding one with a fairly thin mattress which we bought as we had to have something to sleep on.

Later we were to discover the big hypermarkets like Mammouth, Montlaur (which now seems to have disappeared) and Géant Casino where you can buy just about anything at very reasonable prices.

The hypermarkets in France are particularly good for garden furniture. Their prices are a lot lower than in the UK and the quality is good. We made the mistake of passing this information on to our children and subsequently found ourselves travelling with a loaded car in both directions.

We have now bought two double mattresses and numerous large garden tables in hypermarkets. The prices do not vary enormously between the different stores so we tend to go for the one that makes the transport of the item the simplest. In some cases you actually have to take large items, on a trolley, past the checkout. This is not all that easy with a double mattress. The thing that bothers me is that we never see anyone else doing this sort of thing. In the more civilised stores they will give you a bill that you take to the checkout and the large object will be delivered to you outside the checkout area.

I like shopping in the hypermarkets. They have such a wide variety of goods. Even the new superstores in the UK do not come close in the variety of items stocked. I could quite happily spend a couple of hours wandering around Mammouth but I never do. Barbara hates it. As she points out, she goes on holiday for a change, not to spend her time wandering around supermarkets.

Now that I was a resident I thought that I had better report to the *Mairie*, as instructed by Alphonse Pons, and establish my credentials. The only problem was that I had no idea where the *Mairie* was situated.

I walked into the middle of the square and looked around for the *Mairie*. I did not see any building that looked, even remotely, as if it qualified but I did see the village postman disappear up a street at the end of the square. I caught him before he had gone very far.

'Pour La Mairie, s'il vous plaît, monsieur?' I said. He gave me a puzzled look then pointed to the street sign above his head. It read *Rue de La Mairie*. Well at least he had understood my French.

The *Mairie* was a very imposing building, much bigger than I had anticipated. I opened the door expecting to walk into some sort of

MAIRIE

reception area but all I saw was closed doors and a stairway leading upwards. None of the doors had any notices on them so I opted for the stairs. It was a good choice. I could hear voices which I traced to a room at the end of the landing. This was the office. It appeared to be the only room that was actually used for any sort of official purpose. It was a very big *Mairie* to provide a single room for the business of the community. The rest of the building was obviously occupied but not by the *Maire* – he lived in his own house. I suppose it must have been a sort of caretaker. Not a bad job to have as the best house in the village came with it.

As I entered the office I came upon a queue of old ladies. They were all waiting their turn to be dealt with by an efficient looking lady installed behind a long wooden counter.

I joined the end of the queue and the queue vanished as if by magic. The old ladies had formed ranks along the counter and were indicating to me that I should go ahead of them. I protested. They insisted. I looked at the lady behind the counter. She shrugged. I advanced.

'Bonjour, Madame,' I started on my carefully rehearsed speech. *'J'ai acheté une maison dans le village et l'immobilier m'a dit qu'il faut que je vienne ici et vous donne . . .'*

'Ah, oui Monsieur. Quelle maison?' She spoke clearly and not too quickly. Perhaps she had gone to the same school as Alphonse Pons.

The old ladies gathered closer. I now understood their eagerness for me to go first. Very soon the whole village would know all about the newcomers.

'*Numero 8 Rue Renoir*,' I said.

'*Ah, Maison Bonnet*.'

I confirmed that I had indeed bought the house from the Bonnets and now that we had firmly established which property we were talking about it was time to begin the inquisition. She produced a large form.

I had to give my full name and Barbara's full name. That was easy. Then it was our date and place of marriage. I got the place right and made only a small error on the date. I knew my mother's maiden name but when I started to be questioned about my mother-in-law I went into the realms of pure fantasy. How could I possibly be expected to know the full christian names, and, even worse, the maiden name of my mother-in-law.

The old ladies were really loving this and the lady behind the counter seemed to be quite enjoying extracting all this information out of me. She was very pleasant and really quite attractive. We all entered into the spirit of the thing and although the end result may have contained some little inaccuracies there was no harm done and everyone had enjoyed themselves.

When it was all over I was told that I would receive my tax demands in due course. I shook hands with the lady behind the counter, nodded to the old ladies, and escaped.

I later found out that the *Maire* was also an insurance agent. It was a pity that I had given my business to Alphonse Pons as premium renewal time would have provided a nice window of opportunity in such areas as planning permission.

The following morning I went to the *boulangerie*. The same old ladies were there; or at least they looked the same. But this time there was no pushing me to the front of the queue, as I was only there to buy bread not to disclose all my family secrets.

We were now in a position to examine the house in more detail. Yes, it was in *très bon état* but, like all village houses in France, there were damp spots where the wall was crumbling a bit behind the wallpaper or where the paint was flaking a bit. The problem was mainly on the ground floor and the walls concerned were the original walls of the house and at least three feet thick.

It was no real problem as we had decided that the whole house would have to be repapered, not because of the condition of the walls, but because of the design of the wallpaper. We would slap some damp-proof paint on the walls before repapering.

Everything else seemed to be OK.

We had taken a couple of folding chairs down with us and we now decided to venture on to the flat roof and try it out as a terrace.

I climbed up the loft ladder and opened the trap-door. I was momentarily blinded by the bright sunshine. This was great. This was why we had chosen the South of France.

As I have explained previously, the roof has walls on two sides but on the other two sides it is a sheer drop into Rue Renoir and Place de la République respectively.

We positioned ourselves in the safe corner near the trap-door and settled down to enjoy the sun. Even though we were well away from the edge we still felt slightly apprehensive. A wall round the terrace would have to be the top priority.

It was very pleasant on the roof but something was missing. The alarm on my wristwatch going off reminded me what it was. I always have the alarm set for twelve noon, as that is when the sun goes over the yardarm and alcoholic beverages can be consumed by respectable people. I actually tried cheating a little on this by keeping my watch on UK time but Barbara was not fooled. She was quite firm on that point. Eleven a.m. is too early to start drinking even on holiday, except, of course, on special occasions.

I nipped down to the kitchen and got a nice cold bottle of fizzy white wine out of the fridge. *Méthode Champagnoise* but certainly not Champagne. Here we were talking 15 francs a bottle. I stopped off at the *salon* on the way back to collect the bottle of *Crème de Cassis* and the glasses.

A mere spot of *Cassis* in the bottom of the glass and a topping up with cold fizzy white wine gives you a *Kir Royal* which is a very pleasant drink on a warm day. It is well worthwhile buying the slightly more expensive *Crème de Cassis* - about 30 francs a bottle - as it is much better than the cheaper stuff. You can also get *Crème de Framboise, Crème de Fraise, Crème de Mûre* and *Crème de Pêche*. They are all very good if you buy the better quality products. However the only place that I managed to find a really good *Crème de Pêche* was in the duty free shop at Charles de Gaulle Airport, and that cost about 65 francs for a 70 cl bottle.

We had our three glasses each and the bottle was empty. Now I felt a little more daring. I wanted to look down into the square and see what was going on.

I carefully edged my way along the wall of the house next door and with a firm grip on the wall leant forward and peered down into the square. There was not a tremendous amount of activity. There were one or two people sitting outside the *café* and a man was shouting at two little white dogs who ran around yapping. All very tranquil. I relaxed and leant on the side wall and contemplated the drop into the square with a bravado bred of Dutch courage. Just then the silence was shattered by a blast of extremely loud music that seemed to be coming from above my head. I clung on to the wall my knees shaking.

It was 'Lady of Spain' and it lasted for about fifteen seconds. Then there was the sound of someone blowing into a microphone followed by '*Allo, Allo. Le Poissonnier de Pouzins est dans la Place*.' The speaker then gave a long list of all the fish that the fishmonger had to offer and concluded with a few more bars of 'Lady of Spain.'

Allo, Allo is a regular feature of village life. Up to ten mobile shops visit the village in a day and in addition you have all sorts of other announcements ranging from football practice to details of the prize-giving ceremony at the village school.

There are four speakers placed on the clock tower about thirty metres from our terrace. As the message has to reach the whole village the volume is much greater than is necessary to reach us. Still, we have got used to it and we never warn any of our guests about this little surprise.

The earliest they broadcast is about 8 am which is all right unless you have been overdoing it the night before.

CHAPTER 10

Auguste and the Apparition

We only had a couple of days to spend in the village as I had to return to attend a course.

It had been many years since I had attended a course even though there was a company rule that everyone had to do at least two weeks of education every year. This time all my usual tactics had failed as it was considered a very important course. It was a Quality Workshop and our Vice-President had said that he wanted all his key decision makers to attend. Apparently our Japanese competition had discovered quality and now we had to learn what it was all about.

I have got to admit that I was a little flattered to discover that I was considered a key decision maker by the Vice-President. This unfamiliar feeling of importance soon evaporated when I scanned the list and saw the other people who had received a similar invitation to attend.

This Vice-President was American. We called him Delboy because of the amount of jewellery he wore.

My initial impression of Delboy was very favourable. I did my first presentation to him shortly after he arrived. He listened attentively and at the end congratulated me on a fine piece of work. He said the transparencies were particularly good.

A few weeks later I was part of the audience for another presentation. It was badly prepared and the visual aids were dreadful.

At the end Delboy congratulated the presenter on a fine piece of work. He said he was particularly impressed with the transparencies.

Like most Vice-Presidents, Delboy did not stay very long with us but he did make a lasting impression on me with one particular statement he made at a meeting I attended.

'Fifty million dollars is a nit,' he said. Taken in context his statement may well have been quite reasonable. It certainly impressed me. Unfortunately he did not extend the same philosophy to the calculation of our salary increases.

As our time was limited we thought that we had better have a good look around the village.

In addition to the houses in the centre of the village there were around twenty new houses either built or under construction on the outskirts of the village. This was the same in all the villages round about. The new houses were occupied by people who commuted to work in the surrounding towns whereas the majority of people who lived in the village houses either worked in the vineyards or did not appear to work at all.

As we were appreciating the view from our terrace we had seen an imposing looking building on the outskirts of the village so we decided to investigate. We took the road out of the square that looked most likely to lead us to our goal and found ourselves on the Rue de l'Apparition.

The building, or I should say buildings, we came upon after a few hundred metres were indeed impressive. It was the Convent of Notre Dame du Dimanche. In addition to the main building there was a chapel and a shrine. So what was the story of Notre Dame du Dimanche? As usual it was Taff who found an old book on the area that gave us the answer.

In 1870, apparently, many of the vineyards were hit with a deadly scourge called phylloxera which completely destroyed the vines. The first vineyards to be visited by the blight in the general area were in the small valley between St. Crispin and the next village to the south. Nothing strange in that I hear you say, it had to start somewhere. Nothing strange except that shortly before, on that very spot, the Blessed Virgin herself had appeared to forecast a lower than normal harvest that year.

NOTRE DAME DU DIMANCHE

A gentleman called Auguste Arnaud, a citizen of St. Crispin, was doing a bit of digging in his vineyard one Sunday morning while the morning mass was taking place in the village church. He was sitting on the edge of the hole that he had dug enjoying a little rest and a modicum of nourishment. Now nourishment, in this part of the world, seldom means food alone but a little wine hurts nobody and there is nothing on record to suggest that Auguste may have been overindulging on this occasion. Therefore, we have the completely sober Mr. Arnaud, sitting contemplating Montpellier's chances of winning the cup, when suddenly a lady of dazzling beauty, adorned in gold and silver, appears before him. Now Auguste had seen the Mayor's wife dressed up to the nines at the Quatorze Juillet celebrations but this was in another league altogether. It was, without doubt, an apparition.

'Why are you working on a Sunday?' the Lady demanded. 'Can you not see the blight that is coming that will destroy everything. I cannot contain the anger of my son. Cease your work and go and pray!'

Having had her say the apparition then disappeared.

Auguste told the other villagers all about his experience. He must have been held in some regard because not only did they believe him but, at his bidding, they all gathered at the spot where he said the Virgin would appear for a second time.

At the appointed time Arnaud stood at the far end of his vineyard. At the other end was the cross that he had planted by the side of the road where the Virgin had first appeared. Arnaud raised his eyes to the heavens and began to walk across the vineyard towards the cross. It was as if an invisible hand was moving the vines out of his way as he walked straight to the cross without stumbling once. At the cross he fell to his knees and began to pray and when he looked up there was the virgin. She was visible only to Arnaud but when he passed on the message that she wanted the assembled throng to sing the *Magnificat* the 500 voices bellowed forth without hesitation. The die was cast and Notre Dame du Dimanche was conceived.

We bought some old photographs of the village that probably date from the turn of the century. We bought them at the local market from an English couple who have made a business of selling enlarged reproductions of old postcards and photographs. I do not know where they find all their material but they appear to have something on every village in the area. They set up their stall at all the local markets and seem to do quite well. When I approached the stall the chap asked me in French what village I was interested in.

'*St. Crispin de la Forêt*,' I said in my finest French accent. I had practised the pronunciation over and over again and was sure that I had it spot on.

'Try that box over there,' he replied in English.

I do not visit him often enough for him to remember me and one day I am going to get him to reply to me in French.

I visited the *alimentation* in the village. The shelves were crammed full of all sorts of things in no particular order. You had the feeling that absolutely anything that you ever wanted could be found there somewhere and Monsieur Alimentation always knew where to look.

'*Je voudrais un tire-bouchon*,' I said to Madame Alimentation.

I could immediately see that I had caused a great problem. We were the new arrivals in the village and they wanted to demonstrate their ability to meet our every need.

'*Je suis desolé, monsieur, mais nous n'avons pas un tire-bouchon.*'

I looked round the packed shelves and something in my facial expression must have sent the message to Madame Alimentation that a second opinion was needed. Monsieur Alimentation was summoned.

He agreed with his wife. We had caught them out in such a simple, but nevertheless essential, product as a corkscrew.

We had decided to eat *chez nous* that evening. I had put a couple of bottles of *Listel Gris de Gris*, a perfectly acceptable local *rosé* wine, in the fridge and at the appropriate moment had discovered the absence of a corkscrew.

'Never you mind,' I said to Barbara, 'I'll just pop over to the *alimentation* and get one.'

Now I was going to have to return empty handed. It would have to be the cork pushed down into the bottle and all that nonsense.

This was not, however, to be the case. Monsieur Alimentation started out of the shop at a great speed beckoning with his arms and shouting, '*Venez, venez!*'

I followed. He stopped about a hundred yards up a narrow street and banged on a door. As I caught up with him, the first floor window opened and a man stepped out on to the terrace. He had a napkin tucked into his shirt and was holding a piece of bread in his hand. There was a rapid exchange in French that I could not follow but certain words did register. '*Urgent . . .catastrophe . . . Les Anglais*'. I would like to think that the honour of the village had been mentioned but I would be exaggerating if I said so.

The man disappeared and a moment later reappeared at a garage door. In his hand he held a cardboard box full of new shrink wrapped corkscrews. I bought one from him for about the same price that I would have paid in a supermarket. It turned out that he was a producer and seller of wine and people in his line of business also sold corkscrews. That was probably the reason that the *alimentation* did not stock such items. I had not caught them out at all; it was simply a demarcation issue.

I must say that I was impressed by the seriousness with which Monsieur Alimentation had treated my problem. But then it did fall into the most important segment of French life - food and drink.

We headed home the next day having carefully measured key areas of the house. The winter months were not going to be idle. I would make things, like a hob unit, which I would then dismantle for transportation. Barbara would make curtains.

I delivered Barbara to the ferry at Calais and went on to Brussels to attend my course.

CHAPTER 11

I am a Telephone

My company car was due for renewal so I reviewed my requirements in the light of my new acquisition in the South of France.

The car would have to be French to make life simpler in case of breakdowns. This was no problem as I liked French cars anyway. It would have to be able to carry large objects as most of the furniture for the house would come from the UK. An estate car was the obvious choice but Barbara did not like estate cars.

In the end I decided on a Renault 25. It was French. It was a hatchback and it had a lot of boot space. It also spoke to you. It was a great novelty for a while, particulary with aging relatives. I would leave the handbrake slightly on, or a door not quite shut, and the car would, in a slightly pompous tone, advise us of the problem to the great surprise and entertainment of the occupants.

However there was another side to the talking car. It was a bit like that story of the ventriloquist and the dummy. I found myself answering the car. When it told me it was getting a bit low on fuel I would respond with, 'Thank you for letting me know.' On one occasion it told me that my headlights were not working when I could clearly see that they were and I have to confess that I reprimanded the car in no uncertain fashion. The car was silent for a long time after that. Was it my imagination or was it sulking?

The real problem was that there did not appear to be any way to turn the volume down. You could turn it off completely but then you would not get the messages that you actually wanted to hear. The most annoying message was 'LIGHTS ON'. This was an important message when you were leaving the car for a reasonable period but when you were just going to fill up with petrol it was a bit tedious.

Barbara once drew up beside a petrol pump to fill up. It was dark, the car lights were on, she was on her own and the petrol station was quite busy. She was also not in the best of moods. When she stepped out of the car and the car announced to the whole assembled company 'LIGHTS ON', she turned on it and snarled, 'I know the bloody lights are on, I am only going to get petrol.' She suddenly realised what she had done. She looked around her. All the other customers had stopped what they were doing and were observing her with a mixture of amusement and concern - after all we do live near Broadmoor. There was nothing else for it - she got back into the car and went to another garage.

I really quite liked the talking car but there was one occasion when I have to confess that the car disappointed me. I had stopped at traffic lights and another car ran into me from behind at about 30 mph. What did the car say? Absolutely nothing!

I was still spending a lot of time in Paris on business and I used every opportunity that I could to practise my French. This was not too easy as I found that my amateurish efforts did not meet with a great deal of encouragement from the Parisian public.

Parisians are, in my view, incredibly rude and selfish people. When driving in Paris in the rush hour, which is most of the time, you must be very careful not to get into the wrong lane. If you do make this mistake there is little point in indicating that you want to change lanes. The Parisian drivers will just look at you curiously and never even consider letting you into their lane. Your only hope is that another visitor comes along. I used to think that their behaviour was due to the fact that they disliked foreigners but my observations have shown me that they treat each other equally badly.

I once asked a villager in St. Crispin what he thought about British people buying holiday homes in his village.

'Better than Parisians buying them,' he replied.

We had several French assignees in the department so I decided to try out my French on them. They refused to cooperate, however, on the basis that they had come to the UK to learn English, not to teach the English to speak French.

One French lady was moderately helpful until we were having a heated debate in a business meeting and I tried to restore a bit of calm with, *'d'accord, ne dérangez pas vos culottes.'*

I did ask one of my French colleagues why all the English words that the French had adopted like *le football* and *le weekend* were masculine. He said that he felt sure that this was not the case. There must be at least one feminine English word but he could not think of any at that moment.

It took him a while but eventually he returned with a triumphant look on his face.

'*La pin-u*p' he said.

It was with such valuable additions to my vocabulary that I prepared for an extended visit to St. Crispin the following Easter.

Taff and Melanie have a different approach to travelling from us. They will relax with the daily papers on a mid-morning ferry and as soon as they are off the boat in Calais they will decide it is lunchtime and go in search of a nice restaurant. Two-and-a-half hours later they will start their journey south having got themselves completely acclimatised to *la vie française*.

We normally catch an earlier ferry and eat on board so that we can get started on our journey without delay. It has become a habit for us to have the full English breakfast. This, in my case, consists of bacon, double fried egg, fried bread, double sausage and baked beans. It is, of course, very unhealthy eating but as we only do this sort of thing on ferries we are not putting ourselves too much at risk.

Taff had stayed at the *Relais Fleuri* at Avallon on the way down and he recommended it to us.

He also told me that there was a very good restaurant where they always stopped for lunch the following day. He gave me one of the cards from the restaurant which I carefully packed away in my wallet.

Avallon is about 200 kilometres south of Paris which meant that we would have about 550 kilometres to do the next day. The hotel was very comfortable, reasonably priced and handy for the autoroute.

When we saw Taff later in the week we told him that we were pleased with his recommendation.

'And did you stop for lunch in the restaurant I told you about?' he asked.

We had looked at the card as we enjoyed a *digestif* after a pleasant meal at the *Relais Fleuri*. The restaurant was just south of Macon. Now Macon is less than 200 kilometres from Avallon, but then, after a latish rise, and a leisurely *petit déjeuner*, I suppose a couple of hundred kilometres before lunch is not too bad.

'We had lunch on our terrace in St Crispin,' I said.

It took a long time to convince Taff that we were telling the truth. We had left Avallon about 8.30 am and were sitting on our terrace having stopped to buy some essential victuals on the way, at around 2 pm.

Perhaps one day, when all the work on the house is completed, we will learn to relax and travel in a more leisurely fashion.

The weather was not good in St. Crispin de la Forêt. The locals had told us that it was generally pretty good around New Year but Easter could be very cold. Not only was it cold; it was wet.

Fortunately we had some *bois de chauffage*. We also had the very large fireplace in the kitchen with a sort of built-in central heating system. There were two vents on the wall above the fireplace which belted out warm air once you had a good fire going.

We put a heavy curtain across the kitchen door to keep the heat in and reconciled ourselves to living in the kitchen until the weather improved.

We had an electric convector heater for the bedroom so we were not going to freeze to death. Taff had slept in our house for a couple of nights when he was buying his house the previous November. That was before there were any creature comforts like heating. He said that his eyeballs had frozen during the night. I remarked that this was strange as his eyelids should have kept them warm.

'The reason my eyeballs were frozen was because my eyes were wide open,' he explained. 'I was lying there awake, worried about whether I was doing the right thing buying a property in France.'

Our eyeballs were going to remain warm, even if we did awaken during the night, provided we did not have a power cut.

Bois de chauffage is not cheap in France. It costs around 400 francs per cubic metre but it is very well seasoned wood and burns very well.

A much cheaper alternative is to burn the old vines, known as *shish*, which seem to be pulled out each year in large numbers.

The weather did not improve so we were confined to indoor activities of which there were plenty. Removing the violent wallpaper was high on the list of priorities.

Barbara also wanted to do a bit of sewing but discovered that she did not have any needles. After practising pronouncing *aiguille* a few times she set off for the *alimentation*.

Madame Alimentation gave her a warm greeting and listened attentively to Barbara's request. At about the third try, and without having to revert to sign language, the requirement was understood. She delved into one of the overflowing shelves and withdrew a little tin which she handed to Barbara. Barbara began to wonder if the message had in fact got through as she had no idea what was in the tin. She handed Madame a 50 franc note. Madame tut tutted and Barbara thought for a moment that she wanted more money but Madame sorted through he money box and handed Barbara two twenty franc notes, a five franc piece and a half franc. Whatever was in the tin it was not going to be costly mistake.

Sitting in the kitchen Barbara struggled to open the tin. She finally discovered a little bit that slid back and when she shook the tin out came a needle, then another of a different size, then another, then another. There must have been fifty needles in the little tin and they were all in perfect condition. Barbara was convinced that the needle tin was pre-war, partly by the design and partly by the price. Where do you buy fifty needles today for less than 50 pence?

I had decided that railings were the thing for the *toit terrasse* and had seen exactly the sort I wanted in Villemarché on our previous visit. They were outside the *Mairie* and had been recently erected. They were aluminium, quite pleasing to the eye, presumably required no maintenance and most important of all I believed that I could erect them myself.

I thought it worthwhile going into the *Mairie* and asking them who had supplied the railings. Nobody had the faintest idea and as I left I saw them shaking their heads - no doubt they were muttering '*les Anglais*.'

The Building Centre in London had a leaflet on aluminium products including railings from a company called Technal United Kingdom. I suspected that the parent company was, in fact, French and that I was going to be buying railings that had been shipped over from France so that I could ship them back again. As it turned out this was immaterial as it was extremely complicated to work out exactly what bits and pieces were needed in English and it would have tested the most fluent of French linguists to work it out from a French catalogue.

I was a bit concerned about planning permission for the railings. Our house overlooked the main village square and it was possible that the idea of railings, particularly aluminium ones, might not appeal to the *Monsieur le Maire*. I decided to go and see what the Mayor's secretary had to say.

Were they the same old women as last time? It was difficult to tell but once again I was to be the centre of attraction.

'I would like to erect some railings,' I said, 'and I would like to know if I need permission to do so.'

'It is possible,' she said. 'Where are the railings to be erected?'

'On my roof terrace', I replied.

'Why do you need railings?' she asked.

I thought it was time to try for a bit of sympathy.

'To stop myself, my wife and my daughter from falling into La Place de La République,' I replied, keeping a perfectly straight face.

This generated quite a forceful *Oooh là là* from her. The French really do use that expression.

Now I have to confess that only about half the old ladies had been following my conversation and I felt a bit put out that I was not the attraction that I was of old.

The *Oooh là là* drew the other old ladies into the ring.

'You do not have a wall round your terrace?' the secretary asked.

I shook my head.

'And you use it as a terrace?'

I nodded my head.

'That is very dangerous,' she said. 'You should not use it until you have a wall.'

'Or railings,' I suggested.

'Or railings,' she agreed. 'I will have a word with *Monsieur Le Maire* but, first, you must fill in this form.' She handed me a request for planning permission.

In the next few days I saw a lot of the villagers look up at our terrace as they passed. I think they expected to see us sitting at the very edge having our lunch.

Our younger daughter, Roberta, had flown down to spend a few days with us. She was the first member of the family to see our new acquisition and she was suitably impressed.

We did not have a telephone but there were a couple of telephone boxes in the village and they both worked. They did appear, however, to operate a totally different tariff structure. The one by the *Mairie* certainly gave you a lot longer for your five francs than the other one.

It was in the telephone box by the *Mairie* that Roberta was trapped.

She had announced that she was going to the phone box to call her boyfriend. She took all our change, which was not all that much, and disappeared into the drizzle.

Half an hour later we began to get worried as she had certainly not taken enough money for a call to England of this length and it was not the sort of weather for a stroll round the village.

We found her in the telephone box looking out at a medium sized dog that was baring its teeth at her.

We dragged her out and introduced her to the dog which we knew well. He was a very friendly dog but had a deformed lower jaw so that his teeth stuck out and it always looked as if he was snarling.

We decided it was time that we got a phone of our own.

I took Barbara with me when I went to the village PTT office to enquire about having a phone installed. We were leaving in a couple of days so we thought we would arrange for a telephone to be installed during our next visit in a few months time.

I am glad that I took Barbara with me because now she could have some first hand experience of the old ladies.

It was even better in the Post Office for the old ladies because there was a bench to sit on and chat to each other.

We exchanged *bonjours* with the ladies and went to the counter where the village postman greeted us.

I asked if we had come to the right place to arrange for a telephone to be installed. It was about 3.30 pm on a Friday.

The postman looked at his watch.

'I will try,' he said, ' but it may be too late as it is a Friday.'

He picked up the phone and called a number.

He had obviously managed to get through to the right person because he began to ask me questions and to repeat the answers down the phone.

POUSSEZ

After a fairly short period of time he put down the phone.

'Your telephone will be installed next Tuesday morning.' he said, looking very pleased with his efforts. He even told us the telephone number.

'*Parfait*,' I said, '*et merci beaucoup, mais...*'

I then explained that we would be leaving on Monday.

'*Vous avez les voisins*,' he said.

This was perfectly true. We did have neighbours. We had met our neighbour in Rue Renoir when he knocked on our door to tell us that we had stolen his address. As it turned out we had done just that. The estate agent had told us that the address was 8, Rue Renoir and we had passed this address on to utility companies and friends. My neighbour handed me a letter, addressed to me at 8, Rue Renoir. He then pointed to the number above his front door which was also 8. It appeared that we were 8, Place de La République even though our entrance was in Rue Renoir. I was not too unhappy about the change of address as Place de la République sounded rather grand. I was a little concerned that the *Notaire* had used the wrong address, when we bought the house, but the final identifier is always the *cadastre* number which was correct. Our Rue Renoir neighbour was a pleasant enough chap, for a Parisian, but he was not in residence at that time.

The postman saw the hesitation on my face.

'You do not know your neighbours?' he asked.

I explained that the only neighbour I had met was the Parisian.

'*Pas de problème*,' he said. 'We shall ask Monsieur Lagarde.'

He shouted across at the group of old ladies who had, as usual, been enjoying the exciting things that *les Anglais* get up to.

'*Monsieur Lagarde est un très bon homme, n'est-ce pas?*'

Without hesitation the old ladies nodded their agreement and proceed to review the many virtues of the Lagarde family between themselves.

As far as the postman was concerned the episode was closed. Monsieur Lagarde had been selected. It never seemed to occur to anyone that Monsieur Lagarde might not be available next Tuesday morning.

When I knocked on Mr. Lagarde's door and asked him if he would let the telephone man in he said that he would be delighted. He certainly seemed to be a *très bon homme*.

Taff already had a telephone installed when a man from the PTT knocked on his door.

'I have come to install a telephone,' he said.

'*Mais, je suis un téléphone*,' Taff answered.

CHAPTER 12

Au Revoir Pissoir . . . Bonjour Terrasse

If you travel on French autoroutes you will become familiar with the sight, and the sound, of the French private ambulance. Some look like real ambulances but most seem to be private cars and they can be recognised by two things. Firstly they all have a three bar blue cross on the bonnet and the doors. Secondly they always have their beep beepers going as lunchtime approaches.

In late June we were on the *Autoroute du Soleil* heading south at a leisurely 150 kph (90 plus mph) when we felt the urge for a spot of lunch and the use of the *toilette*. The speed limit on the French autoroutes is 130 kph in dry conditions and 110 kph when it is raining. As there is raining and raining, I have been told that the clincher is whether or not you are using your windscreen wipers. I have never tested this theory by overtaking a French police car at 130 kph when it is raining *chats et chiens* with windscreen wipers at rest but I must admit I do regularly break the speed limit.

The fastest I have driven in France is about 175 kph but that was on the almost deserted autoroute to Calais and in retrospect I wonder why I bothered because the ferries run every hour and a half. In general I travel around 150 kph and take the usual precautions to avoid one of these nasty on-the-spot fines. I make sure that I know which is the last exit before each *Péage* and travel at a sedate 130 kph from that point as the favourite trick of the *Gendarmarie* is to set up a radar trap on the last stretch and phone forward to their colleagues who grab you as you stop to pay the toll.

I also have the theory that the French police consider the British to be pretty law-abiding as far as speeding is concerned, unlike the Germans, the Swiss and, of course, the Mercedes class French who consider 200 kph a reasonable cruising speed.

Back to ambulances. As we drove into the service area we noticed that we were being followed by one of the proper looking French ambulances and when we parked it pulled up alongside us.

The ambulance crew, a man and a woman, followed us into the cafeteria and we found ourselves sitting a few tables away from them as we dined. They each had a well filled baguette sandwich which they were consuming enthusiastically but between them was another sandwich wrapped up in the fashion of a *plat à emporter*. 'There is someone in the ambulance', we thought, 'and the sandwich is for the poor patient who is too incapacitated to come inside.'

We wanted to see if this was the case so we waited until they had finished their sandwiches and then we followed them outside.

They went straight to the ambulance and opened the back door. The man climbed aboard and a moment later a sort of mobile stretcher began to appear out of the ambulance. As soon as the stretcher was on the ground they both took hold of the patient, who appeared to be covered from head to foot in bandages. They gradually negotiated the patient into a vertical position which was not easy as the patient, as if encased in a full-lenght plaster cast, did not seem to be able to bend in the middle. It was a matter of digging the patient's heels into the soft grass at the edge of the picnic area and pushing the patient upright. I have to keep saying patient as, at this stage, it was impossible to tell whether we were observing a man or a woman.

The ambulance crew had now managed to gain the attention of quite a few of the families who, enjoying a picnic, were observing the antics with increasing interest. Knives and forks became motionless as the ambulance man produced a bottle and held it halfway down the front of the patient. It was now fairly safe to assume that the patient was a man. When the patient had finished relieving himself, the ambulance man emptied the contents of the bottle onto the ground. Perhaps regulations demand that a bottle is used but in this case it seemed a bit redundant. The bottle was certainly not used to spare the patient embarrassment because, if that had been the objective, the ambulance crew would have faced him away from the large audience of picnickers.

When this was over the ambulance lady waved the jambon et fromage baguette at the patient and they all disappeared inside the ambulance. I hope the patient enjoyed his sandwich.

One of the things that had influenced us in buying a house in a small French village was the feeling that, no matter how long it was before our next visit, things would always be the same.

When we arrived back in St. Crispin we discovered that the *alimentation* had changed hands and the *pissoir* had disappeared.

An examination of the *alimentation* was not encouraging. It was spotlessly clean and all the goods were arranged in a logical sequence. You could find what you wanted quite easily. There was even a proper till that produced printed receipts. It was not the same.

The *pissoir* had been replaced by an earth-filled stone trough in which flowers had been planted. It looked very pleasant, but a French village has to have a proper *pissoir*.

I took this up with Roger, the husband of the *café* owner, as we sat at one of the tables in the square.

'It is a great shame that the *pissoir* has gone,' I said.

He did not agree. He thought that the flower bed was a great improvement.

'But a French village must have a *pissoir*.' I argued.

'The village does have a *pissoir*,' he said. 'It is next to the PTT.'

My French was not up to discussing with him the reasons why people who went to the Post Office might require the use of a *pissoir*, whereas, it was obvious that his clientele would find one quite useful from time to time.

As if to prove my point, one of his customers wandered over to the tree in the middle of the square and relieved himself.

Roger watched him then turned to me and shrugged. You see there was no problem. Things always sorted themselves out.

I exaggerate when I say that his customers required the regular use of a toilet because apparently they drank very little. It was our custom to wander over to the *café* after our evening meal for a *café cognac*. If all the tables were occupied Roger would find us a table, one way or another, because we were paying customers.

CAF
OMME

I would look round the other tables and if there was a drink in sight it would be very unusual. Perhaps they had all bought drinks before we arrived. On the very few occasions when I did see a drink being purchased it was a small glass of beer, and I mean small. It was not a *demi* which is 25 centilitres, but a little glass, with a stem, that looked about half the size of a *demi*.

There were three distinct groups of people who frequented the *café*.

First of all there were the regulars, the old hands, who were, almost to a man, non-buyers of drinks. They were in the age group of 40 upwards. One chap was always the worse for wear, but he must have arrived in that state because he was never seen to put any business the way of the *café* owner. I suppose it is not unreasonable, if you are a bit strapped for cash and have a plentiful supply of wine at home, to have a few before venturing forth to socialise with your friends at the *café*. Despite the fact that this group seldom bought a drink, we never saw the slightest pressure put on them to vacate their tables. In fact it was quite the opposite. Roger would wander around chatting to them and evidently keeping them company in the non-consumption of alcohol as I never saw him with a drink in his hand either.

The second group were the youngsters. They would roar up in their Peugeot 205 GTI's or on their motor bikes, kiss all their friends, stay for ten minutes and then roar off again. If they did buy a drink, which was also unusual, it would be a soft drink of some revolting colour.

Then there were the expatriates and the visitors. This was the group that bought the drinks. Even the foreigners who lived in the village all year round, like the English carpenter and his wife, would never be without a drink if they were sitting at one of the tables.

Most evenings in the summer we would have a walk round the village before settling down for our *café cognacs* at the *café*.

We would stop and watch the *pétanque* players as they competed with great seriousness, amongst the plane trees, on the specially illuminated patch of land next to the *Mairie*.

I had said to Taff one day, as we were discussing village life in the Languedoc over a glass of wine, that we often watched the *boule* players in the evening.

'I think you will find that they are playing *pétanque* and not *boules*,' he responded.

'*Ah bon*,' I said, not really believing him and made a mental note to investigate this important issue further.

He was absolutely right. *Boules* is a game where you release your *boule* when moving up to a particular spot; a bit like British bowls. In *pétanque*, which uses slightly smaller *boules* you stand with your feet together when you throw. *Pétanque* actually means 'feet together.' The game of *boules* was officially declared a sport by the French government in 1982 but *pétanque* has yet to receive such recognition.

In the village the really good *pétanque* players seemed to have two things in common. They always had a cloth to dust the balls while they were awaiting their turn and their boule throwing arm seemed to be slightly deformed. It was shorter than the other arm and the back of the hand always faced forward even when they were walking along the street. The best player, by far, was old Monsieur Carrière. He must have been around seventy and one of his great pleasures was to demonstrate his skill at the village *fête* where prizes were to be won by breaking bottles with *boule*s.

Old Monsieur Carrière would break bottle after bottle and collect his prizes. The stall owner did not really mind because Monsieur Carrière made it look so easy. This encouraged lots of other people to have a go, particularly the young Peugeot 205 GTI drivers who had no skill with the *boules* but wanted to impress their girlfriends. They were usually unsuccessful and when the queue had dispersed and things quietened down old Monsieur Carrière would return to set the whole sequence in motion again.

We saw Philippe, the son of the *café* owner being given lessons (on one of our first visits to the *pétanque* pitch) and he must have been a promising student because a few months later he was involved in one of the serious matches complete with *boule* dusting cloth.

We had brought the railings down with us in the back of the car. First we would have to assemble them, then attach them securely to the roof. When that was done we would have a proper terrace.

We had received permission, by default, to put up the railings. The planning application form had been fairly easy to complete but I also had to send off three copies of drawings showing the before and after. I carefully drew a plan of the house, exactly to scale, with and without railings. When I say exactly to scale that is an exaggeration. Nobody, not even an architect, could draw a completely accurate plan of the house because there are no right angles and no straight walls. In fact the curves on some of the walls are quite dramatic. This precluded the use of normal skirting board. The previous occupants had used a sort of rubber skirting board that we were not too keen on. We were not sure about what to replace this with until Barbara had a great idea.

'We have lots of old tiles,' she said. 'We could cut them in two and stick them round the walls, just mixing up the designs.'

Of course, we did not have all that many six by six tiles but we discovered that we could buy odd ones for virtually nothing. There was no problem sticking them round the uneven walls and the end result was very pleasing to the eye.

I took some photocopies of my vaguely accurate plans at the local estate agents for five francs a go. The planning authority must have been satisfied with my efforts because I received an acknowledgment within a couple of weeks saying that if I did not hear anything further, by such and such a date, I could assume that permission was granted. I did not hear anything further so I went ahead and ordered the railings.

The design of the railings was extremely clever. There was a top bar and a bottom bar with slots in them. The uprights fitted into these slots and were pinned in position. This was not a very difficult exercise but incredibly noisy; however as the French seem to totally ignore noise this was not really a problem. Every metre or so, instead of an upright, you cut a larger hole and insert a post. The posts fit into feet that bolt to the concrete roof.

The problem was that there was no margin for error. The feet had to be bolted into the concrete in exactly the right spot.

Each of the feet required two holes to be bored about four inches deep for the expanding bolts. This was not easy as the concrete was very tough. It was very hot and I had to work right at the edge of the roof. After a lot of trial and error I eventually decided that the best approach was to use a small drill, then a bigger one and finally the required size of drill. This was a lot of drilling using a hammer drill and I thought that even the French might cast a disapproving eye up at the roof, but there was no sign of this. The sweat began dripping off the end of my nose with ever increasing rapidity. I discovered that a little lubrication helped the drilling so I carefully directed the drips into the drill holes. Ever since I worked in Organisation and Methods many years ago I have been accused by Barbara of being the least well organised person in the World. On this occasion I think I demonstrated my true O & M skills.

The railings were assembled in four sections. Each section was about three metres in length and even though they were aluminium they were quite heavy.

The feet for the first section were in place. Barbara and I picked up the railing and moved slowly towards the edge of the roof. We stood there with the section of railing poised over the feet swaying back and forth in an effort to get the posts in line with the holes. Before we had time to start worrying about the sheer drop the totally unexpected happened. The railing slid neatly into place.

I was careful not to become *blasé* after my initial success and used the same care in measuring the location of the feet for the other three sections. Soon all four sections of railing were in place and bolted down. We had a terrace.

We celebrated by cracking open a bottle of the local *vin mousseux brut* and stood with our *kir royals*, leaning on the railings and, for the first time, had a really good look around the village.

It was from the vantage point of the terrace, a few days later, that we saw Vikki, our elder daughter, her husband, Clive and 5 week-old Charlotte arrive.

Charlotte was a great hit with the old ladies. They all wanted to know her name, which they immediately changed to Carlotta.

CHAPTER 13

A Chilling Reception at the Vieux Logis

The ferry was very busy for the crossing to Calais in early September. The sun was shining out of a clear blue sky so, no doubt, this had attracted a lot of day trippers. There were also a large number of Japanese schoolgirls.

Children of school age travelling en-masse on cross channel ferries is something that the ferry companies really should warn you about. It should be printed on the tickets. 'This is a Government Health Warning. You may come across groups of schoolchildren, apparently unsupervised, during the crossing. Tests have shown that such encounters can damage your sanity.'

The Japanese girls were extremely well-behaved. I remember wondering whether Japanese boys would conduct themselves in such an exemplary fashion and it suddenly occurred to me that I had never seen a group of Japanese boys travelling abroad although I had certainly seen groups of girls before. Perhaps there is something in the Japanese culture that forbids the male of the species from leaving his native soil until he has attained his majority, or possibly he has to qualify in some other way. Could it be that he has to own a certain number of cameras, or, even more to the point, prove that he has the stamina to carry them around with him for a full day's sight-seeing?

The more mature Japanese have certainly shown themselves to be very professional travellers. Based upon their experience abroad I am surprised that they do not achieve greater fame in the game of rugby. They have a natural instinct to form a ruck particularly when approaching any form of *chicane* in an airport and there is very little one can do to stop them when they get some momentum up.

There is a theory that one third of the population of Japan has to be travelling abroad at any point of time as the country is not big enough to hold all of them.

The schoolgirls took a lot of photographs of each other and very little of anything else. Most of them wore glasses and the particular group that we were observing had only one girl, out of about ten, that did not wear glasses. When it was her turn to be photographed a very strange thing happened. She turned to one of the other girls and borrowed a pair of glasses for the photograph.

When we arrived at the village we discovered that the main square had been cordoned off.

We had to go all the way round the outskirts of the village and eventually managed to park fairly close to the house which was just as well as we had the usual full load.

When we rounded the corner into the square we saw that Monsieur Lagarde and several of the other villagers were congregated outside the *Crédit Agricole* watching the activity in the square.

We put down our suitcases and wandered over to exchange *bonjours* and find out what was going on.

'It is the annual *fête*,' Monsieur Lagarde said.

'Good.' I said. 'We have arrived just in time.'

'Perhaps,' he replied. 'It is an experience.'

Monsieur Lagarde did not seem to be too taken with the idea of the annual *fête* and a little later that day we would understand why.

The ladies wanted to know about Carlotta and after we had assured them that all was going well with the family we headed for *chez nous*.

The first thing we did was rush up to the terrace to have a good look at what was going on. There was, after all, no point in having the best vantage point in the village if we were not going to make use of it.

The whole of the square was a hive of activity as preparations were being made for the big evening. A stage was being constructed out of scaffolding, and enormous loudspeakers were being connected up on either side. They were the largest loudspeakers that I had ever seen. In front of the stage was a space, presumably for dancing, and beyond that, outside the *café*, long tables had been set up. Perhaps the *café* relied upon making most of their annual revenue on this one evening.

There were also several large marquees being erected but we could not see what was going on inside them.

We decided that we would go to the *fête* after we had been out to dinner that evening. This was exciting stuff and we were in high spirits as we unpacked our car even though we had to walk four times as far as usual with our loads.

The restaurant we always went to on our first night down south was the Auberge du Vieux Logis. It was traditional French cooking at its very best and their guinea fowl casserole was out of this world. Naturally, as it was so good, it has now closed down. I suppose it was inevitable, really, as they had no idea how to attract business. The restaurant was on the outskirts of Villemarché but in a secluded area and what signs there were to advertise it were pretty insignificant and not too good on directions. The restaurant consisted of a kitchen, a large dining room and another room about half the size that was not used. I once walked into this unused room when looking for the waiter and discovered that it had a large picture window with a magnificent view of the river which flowed past the restaurant. Perhaps they thought that the view would distract the diner from the full enjoyment of the food.

Another problem was that you never knew if they would be open. They were fairly consistent during the high season but once you got to mid-September you just had to go and find out for yourself. I did try phoning but gave that up having been assured that the restaurant was open only to discover on arrival that it was closed. I once saw Kevin, who was the head waiter and also the son of the owner, doing some shopping in the local supermarket in Villemarché. We called him Kevin because he bore a striking resemblance to Kevin Keegan. We had been to the restaurant the previous evening to discover that it was closed so I collared him and asked if he planned to open the restaurant that evening.

'Of course,' he answered. 'Am I not buying provisions for the kitchen at this very moment?'

The restaurant did not open that evening even though Kevin seemed to be in no doubt earlier in the day that it would. I think they must have had some sort of ritual they practised shortly before opening time and if the omens were not good they just packed up and went home.

On this occasion the restaurant was open but then it was still early September and the tourist season was not quite over. As it was a very warm evening, we sat out on the terrace. We ordered a bottle of *Picpoul de Pinet* from Kevin and settled down to study the menu.

Our elder daughter who had been to the Vieux Logis after we had left earlier in the summer had told us that a new trainee waiter had been taken on. She said that we should watch out for him as, although he was very enthusiastic, he did tend to be a little bit on the clumsy side.

'That must be him,' Barbara said nodding her head at a young waiter who was walking around replenishing the bread baskets on the tables.

We watched him for a while. He even seemed to be taking orders from the diners which is something that Kevin did not normally delegate.

As he disappeared into the doorway behind our table, Barbara, who is a great defender of the oppressed turned to me.

'He seems perfectly OK to me.' she said. 'Obviously he has learned a lot during the past few weeks. I really wish our daughter would not make these snap judgements about people.'

Just then the young waiter came round the corner carrying two jugs of iced water in each hand. As he passed the door his cuff caught in the door handle and he poured the full contents of two of the jugs down Barbara's back. The young waiter was mortified. He rushed off to get some napkins to dry Barbara out. By the time he came back Barbara had got over the initial shock and was able to laugh about it. He looked very relieved that she was taking it so well. He was probably still on probation.

'Anyone could make a mistake like that,' Barbara said when he had gone. She was unwilling to give up her cause even after her chilling experience.

'Here he comes again,' I said to Barbara a few minutes later. 'This time he has a big tureen of hot soup.'

There was a brief look of panic on Barbara's face and in spite of herself I could see her shoulders hunch up ever so slightly.

AUBERGE
DU
VIEUX LOGIS
RESTAURANT

'You are a swine,' she said as the waiter passed carrying nothing more innocuous than a *salade mixte*.

The meal was excellent and we were in a very happy frame of mind as we made our way back to the village and the delights of the annual *fête*.

Parking was difficult but we managed to find a spot by the sole remaining village *pissoir* next to the Post Office. Judging by the number of cars the village *fête* was a very popular event.

It was a warm evening and Barbara had completely dried out so we wandered along to see what delights awaited us in the village square.

There was a DJ up on the stage surrounded by the usual array of equipment and the loudspeakers were blaring out the popular tunes of the day. Quite a few people were dancing but a lot more were sitting at the tables outside the *café*. This time they all had glasses in front of them and they were enjoying themselves in a boisterous fashion.

There were also a lot of people trying their luck at the various stalls. We decided to have a look at what they were up to and discovered that the largest of the marquees housed several roulette tables. It was a somewhat simplified version of roulette and it was very popular.

The only person I recognised was my next door neighbour. This was not Monsieur Lagarde but the chap on the other side. He was a very friendly fellow and I had exchanged the odd pleasantry with him from time to time. He had a large pile of chips in front of him and the maniacal look in his eyes of the compulsive gambler. He gave us a friendly nod but made it clear that he was engaged in serious business and did not want to be disturbed.

I made a few bets to no avail and, as Barbara does not approve of gambling, we wandered off. Well, it is not exactly true to say that Barbara does not approve of gambling. She just does not approve of losing.

We sat outside the *café* with our coffees and our cognacs and watched the dancing. It would have been nicer if the music had not been so loud but the ambition of the young to permanently damage their eardrums apparently knows no frontiers.

Around midnight we decided it was time to go home.

Just before we went to bed we had a look at the scene in the square from the terrace. The *fête* was still in full swing. Even then we did not fully appreciate how loud the music was.

It was only when we were lying in our bed that we started thinking decibels. It was impossible to sleep. Normally a reasonable amount of wine and cognac will guarantee sleep but not on this occasion.

We tried closing the window even though it was still very warm. The music was not quite so loud but the window vibrated to the beat which made it even more difficult to sleep.

Around two o'clock the music stopped but by then we were too shell shocked to get straight off to sleep.

The following morning I met Monsieur Lagarde in the square.

'Did you enjoy the *fête*?' he asked with a smile.

'Yes it was very good,' I replied. 'But the music was so loud that we could not get to sleep.'

'That is the problem of having a house on the square,' he said.

'At least we can sleep well tonight,' I said.

'Ah you do not know?' he laughed. 'The *fête* is on tonight as well.'

We stayed long enough to witness the *vendange* for the first time.

Quite a few strangers appeared in the village to help with the grape harvest. There was a group of Polish men who, we were told, rented a house in the village every year for the period of the *vendange*. They worked hard to accumulate as much money as possible which they used to buy digital watches to take back to Poland.

The villagers would start up their tractors at around 6.30 a.m. They would then drive them out of their *caves* into the square and leave them there with the engines running for about fifteen minutes, presumably while they went indoors for a last cup of coffee. Small crowds of grape pickers would gather and shout at each other over the noise of the tractors. Transport would arrive, horns blaring, to attract the attention of the grape pickers. They would clamber noisily aboard and take off for the vineyards. After a while the tractors would follow and peace would return to the square.

September, we decided, was not a good time to visit the village if your objective was to catch up on lost sleep.

The *vendange* is very different depending upon the type of grapes grown.

For dessert grapes the *patron* has a van that accommodates a certain number of large tubs. The pickers fill the tubs, presumably taking a certain amount of care not to damage the grapes, and these are transported to one of many temporary packing stations set up in the village. Tables are set up in *caves* throughout the village and the older family members sit around chatting whilst sorting and packing the grapes. They are, no doubt, very happy that they have attained the age where they can sit in the shade rather than having to pick the grapes in the hot sun.

Those who grow grapes for wine drive tractors which pull large metal trailers. When the trailer is filled it is driven to the *Cave Cooperative* where the grapes are dumped into a trough for weighing before being crushed.

During the *vendange* the roads are always crowded with slow-moving tractors. It is not advisable to try to go anywhere around five in the evening as all the tractors are heading for all the *Cave Cooperatives* with their final load of the day around that time.

I suppose it must be a very satisfying time for all the vineyard owners as they finally see some return for all their efforts during the year. When the villagers return from their grape picking they certainly look worn out but, at the same time, in very good spirits.

CHAPTER 14

The Wheel of Misfortune

As soon as we arrived in the village on the 28th of December we noticed the small table covered by a black cloth. On the table lay an open book. The table had been placed just outside the front door of the house next to Monsieur Lagarde.

We had never actually seen this sort of set-up before, but you did not have to be too bright to work out that a death had occurred.

We assumed that it was the old lady who had died. She had lived there with her son with whom we had a nodding acquaintance. We had often seen him barbecuing on his terrace which was below ours. We had also seen the old lady on several occasions on the terrace, but never outside the house. I liked the old lady because she had given me a big smile when she thought that I was taking a photograph of her. Well, to be accurate, I was taking a photograph of her but the primary subject matter of the photograph was my newly erected railings on the terrace. She just happened to be leaning over the railings of her terrace at the appropriate moment.

We saw the son dressed in sombre garb and concluded that it was, indeed, the old lady that had died.

People began to arrive to pay their respects. They would stop by the book and sign their names before going into the house. Although many of the people who visited the house were villagers whom we recognised, there were a substantial number of strangers. Considering the fact that we spent most of our time on our terrace, with a good view of their house, and had never seen anyone visit the house before, we were very surprised at the number of outsiders who arrived. Many of them drove expensive cars and obviously enjoyed a very different lifestyle from the family of the deceased.

We did not know quite what to expect in terms of a village funeral so we decided to observe the proceedings from an unobtrusive position.

The arrival of the coffin caught us a bit by surprise. A very old battered van drew up outside and a couple of strangers got out. They opened up the back and pulled out a very nice looking wooden coffin complete with brass fittings. Just like one would expect at home except for the means of transportation.

Through the windows we could observe the progress of the coffin up the stairs. The staircase was obviously very narrow because the coffin had to be carried almost vertical in order to negotiate the stairs. Eventually it was done but we did wonder how they would manage on the return journey with a passenger on board.

The men returned to the van and drove off.

The next thing that happened was that one of the villagers appeared pushing a rusty old trolley. This was normally used to transport the tubs of grapes around but, as we were about to learn, could also serve another purpose.

A heavy velvet cloth was brought out of the house and draped over the trolley. Then the coffin was brought down, with not too much difficulty I am glad to report, and placed on the trolley. After that the whole thing was covered in flowers and the final effect was absolutely marvellous.

The mourners all assembled and followed the trolley as it was pushed round to the church.

A great deal of expense had been spared but the old lady had been given a very nice and very dignified send-off.

On New Year's Day we went to Sète, a nearby fishing port with a large number of restaurants. It is, in fact, the biggest French fishing port on the Mediterranean. The large fishing boats tie up at the quay alongside the restaurants and you can watch them come and go as you enjoy a pleasant lunch. The boats come in two types. There are the *thoniers* which, not surprisingly, fish for tuna and the trawlers that are called *chalutiers*. There are also many small boats owned by the inshore fishermen.

It was a beautiful clear sunny day and we were determined that we would sit outside a restaurant for lunch.

Sète gets very crowded in the high season and it was not exactly empty at New Year. We were obviously not the only people who had selected Sète as a good spot for a *Nouvelle Année déjeuner*.

They have a one way system in Sète which I have never really mastered. Not for the first time I found myself crossing the bridge in the wrong direction but I got away with it and drove down into the large underground car park.

The exit from the car park took us into the street alongside the harbour where most of the restaurants are located. We walked along looking at the menus, all of which offer a multitude of fish courses for a very reasonable price. There is not a great deal of difference in the menus, which always makes selecting a restaurant difficult, so in the end we opted for the one that appeared to be the busiest.

There was nobody sitting outside the restaurant but the tables were laid for lunch so we sat down. Very soon others joined us as it only takes one set of idiots to start a trend. The weather was actually quite pleasant. It was only towards the end of the meal that it became a little chilly but a cognac with the coffee soon warmed us up.

After lunch we went for a walk along the beach. This time our example did not attract any followers. We were the only people on the beach as far as the eye could see.

On the way home we passed over a very rough stretch of road on the outskirts of Sète. There was a loud clanging noise from the back of the car. I thought that I must have run over something and it had got caught under the car so I pulled over to the side of the road.

As I walked round to the rear of the car the reason for the noise was immediately apparent. The cradle that holds the spare wheel was dragging on the ground. It was also empty. Someone had stolen my spare wheel while the car had been parked in the underground car park.

Releasing the spare wheel from outside the car is not a difficult thing to do in a Renault 25. What you cannot do is reconnect the cradle. All you can do is push it upwards where it will remain until the first major bump - then it will fall down again.

I suppose I should have reported the theft to the police and I would have done so had I known the French for spare wheel. I did not have my dictionary with me and by the time I was able to consult a dictionary I would be in St. Crispin. I did not think that the Villemarché police would be willing to mount a major exercise to recover a spare wheel nicked in a seaside resort many kilometres distant.

When I did refer to the dictionary I discovered that someone had stolen my *roue de secours*.

We had brought a couple of bottles of whisky with us as gifts. One was for Monsieur Lagarde and one for a gentleman that we called Monsieur St. Crispin.

Monsieur St. Crispin was not very old, somewhere in his mid-fifties I would say, and he did not appear to do any work. He lived up Rue Renoir and spent most of his time sitting in the square.

Just opposite our house is a tree with a small circular wall round it. Monsieur St. Crispin would sit on the wall with his two little white dogs at his feet. One of the little dogs had long hair and the other short hair. It was the short-haired dog that was a bit of a menace. It would yap at anyone who passed by and chase after them down the square. It never actually tried to bite anyone to my knowledge but always managed to give the impression that a bite could be a distinct possibility.

I parked my car under the same tree so the little white dog and I soon became acquainted. Monsieur St. Crispin attempted to call the dog to heel without any success but the dog soon got tired of me when someone more interesting passed by.

'What is his name?' I asked Monsieur St. Crispin. I was just being sociable but also, it did occur to me that if I could call the little cur by its name it might treat me with a bit more respect.

'St. Crispin,' he said.

My immediate reaction was that he had misunderstood my question and that he thought I had asked the name of the village. On the other hand he knew that I lived in the village. The French consider *les Anglais* to be very strange but surely not strange enough to have to ask the name of the village each morning.

Seeing my puzzled expression he offered an explanation.

'He was born on the same day as St. Crispin's Saints Day.' he said. 'So I called him St. Crispin.'

The gentleman was known as St. Crispin from that point on and we still do not know his correct name.

Monsieur St. Crispin had a little moped with a carrier bag on each side. He did not go out much but when he did he would put a dog in each carrier bag and off he would go with the two little white heads poking out of the bags.

I think the only place he went on the moped was his allotment. He would come back laden with vegetables and soon after there would be a knock on our door and he would give us a carrier bag full of freshly picked produce. It was the same when the dessert grapes came to be picked. He gave us far more than we could possibly eat.

Madame St. Crispin was a different kettle of fish. She was the only person in the village who seemed to be somewhat antagonistic towards us. As we sat on our terrace, on a warm summer evening, we would listen to the voices of the villagers as they sat under the tree in the square. Hers was the only voice we ever heard complaining about *les Anglais* and *les Américains*.

I felt that I had to return Monsieur St. Crispin's generosity but I had to be very careful not to offend him. I thought a bottle of whisky at New Year could not possibly cause offence.

As he passed my house I opened the door and called to him.

'Wait a moment,' I said. 'I have something for you.'

I returned with the bottle of whisky.

'*Je suis Écossais, pas Anglais*,' I said. '*Et j'ai une bouteille d'Eau de Vie Écossais pour vous*.'

He thanked me profusely and wandered off with his prize.

The following morning Madame St. Crispin wished us *bonjour* and gave us a beaming smile. I have often wondered about the exact reason for the transformation. A simple explanation would be that she had a taste for whisky but there are many other possibilities. Perhaps her husband had one too many, fell asleep and she was able to watch what she wanted to on television. My favourite theory is that the whisky had rekindled the flame of desire in Mr. St. Crispin and they had enjoyed a night of unbridled passion.

'*Ce n'est pas nécessaire*,' Monsieur Lagarde said when I had done my little speech for him and offered him the whisky. After a little pressing he accepted and I felt I had done a little to cement Anglo - French relations for the New Year.

We had now owned our house for about fifteen months and had not, so far, received any demand for *impôts locaux*.

In the UK we would not be at all concerned about not receiving a rates demand. We would, in fact, be delighted. But in France we had this horrible feeling that there was something that we had not done and, therefore, we were responsible for there being no rates demand. They would eventually find out and either fine us a large amount or throw us in jail.

I discussed this with Barbara and we decided that the sensible thing to do was for me to go round to the *Mairie* and have a word with the nice lady.

The first thing that I noticed when I entered the office of the *Maire* was the absence of the old ladies. Perhaps at this time of year they did not venture out into the cold winter weather.

The secretary to the *Mairie* seemed genuinely pleased to see me and commented on the fact that I now had a fully serviceable terrace. There could have been a slight hint that she had played a part in the granting of the planning permission so I thanked her for her assistance in the enterprise.

I changed the subject.

'It is over a year since I bought my house,' I said, 'but I still have not had a rates demand.'

'*Ah Monsieur*,' she responded. 'I know nothing of this. It is the responsibility of the *Percepteur de Pouzins*.'

'And where do I find the *Percepteur de Pouzins*?' I asked.

'At *Le Pouzins*, of course, *Monsieur*.'

Le Pouzins had been one of the villages that we had visited when looking for a house so we knew where to go. It is quite a large village so I suppose it is not surprising that the *Percepteur*, whatever a *Percepteur* is, is situated there.

We arrived in Le Pouzins and looked for the sort of large, imposing, building that would house a *Percepteur*.

We found such a building. It seemed to be a *Mairie* plus all sorts of other things. As we wandered around we saw many signs but none that said *Percepteur*. We opened one door and discovered a full orchestra of school children giving a passing rendering of some vaguely familiar classical piece.

When we found some sign of life we enquired after the *Percepteur* and were directed to the other end of the village. We followed the

PERCEPTEUR

directions carefully but could see nothing that looked even remotely like the office of a *Percepteur*.

Then Barbara saw the sign. A small brass plate on the door of a very ordinary looking village house. We knocked on the door and opened it. There was a tiny office that seemed to be stuffed with papers and a very ordinary looking man sitting behind a desk. He did not fit our idea of a *Percepteur* at all. He also seemed very surprised to be receiving visitors.

'*Bonjour*,' I said. 'I have not received a tax demand.'

The look I got was akin to the sort of look an Inspector of Taxes would give you in the UK if you went into his office and said that he had undercharged you on income tax.

I convinced him that I was being serious. I explained where my house was and how long ago I had bought it.

He did not consult any papers.

'*C'est pas pressé*,' he said, giving me a reassuring smile. Well if he was in no hurry then neither were we. We had done our duty in reporting the oversight so we felt exonerated and took our leave of him with a clear conscience.

We have since had a great deal of correspondence with the gentleman. He sends us bills and we send him cheques. There are two types of local taxes, we discovered. The owner of the property pays the *Taxes Foncières* and the occupier the *Taxe d'Habitation*. As we were owners and occupiers we had to pay them both but in the first year the total bill only amounted to around £150 so this was no great cause for concern. The next year was much the same, as was the following year but when we got our rates demand for the third year we found that the total amount had suddenly leapt to over £300. This was no joke, so with the aid of my French dictionary I composed a letter, not to my old chum, the *Percepteur de Pouzins*, but to the *Centre des Impôts Fonciers* in Montpellier. Apparently the *Percepteur* is just a collector of taxes and has nothing to do with how the amount is calculated. We wrote on the 28 January and got a reply in late April.

The explanation was very simple. Two years previously we had filled in a Form H1 that had been sent to us. This form required us to give details of the number of rooms in the house that were habitable and the floor area. It was a simple job to measure one floor, multiply by four and fill in the form. The previous owners had probably done the same calculation but conveniently forgotten the multiplication part. As far as the tax office was concerned we had increased the habitable area by a considerable amount. We were now paying the correct amount of tax but had obviously got off light in the past two years. The reason why it had taken so long for the increase to come through was that you get two years exemption from the higher charge when you make improvements to your house.

Taxes can vary quite considerably from village to village. Houses are given a rateable value and there are three charges made against this value. One for the Region, one for the Department and one for the Commune or village. In our case the percentages are 1.1 for the Region, 6.4 for the Department and 13.4 for the Commune. A friend of mine who has a much larger house in a much smaller village is only charged 3.5 per cent for the Commune.

We were sitting waiting for the ferry at Calais. It was early January so we really did not expect there to be too many coaches.

One coach rolled up alongside and we paid very little attention. Another couple arrived and I gave casual glance in their direction. A notice in the window said 'Glasgow Rangers Supporters Club.'

I said nothing to Barbara who was busy reading the map to see where we had just come from. She takes the rôle of navigator very seriously but not necessarily in the sequence that is most beneficial to the driver.

The arrival of the coach had not registered with her.

Three more coaches pulled up. All bore the same legend.

'Oh my God.'

Barbara had tuned in to what was happening and as she became aware the trickle became a deluge. In all we counted forty-three coaches of potential football hooligans.

'We will catch the next ferry,' Barbara declared in a decisive tone.

'It will be OK,' I said, even though I had very little faith in the sentiment. Glasgow was my home town. I, more than most, was aware of the lively way in which a Glasgow football supporter can celebrate a victory or drown his sorrows after a defeat.

I convinced Barbara that we should take the ferry.

We got on board and went to the bar as usual. We never have a full meal on the way home as we save ourselves for a slap-up Indian meal on our first evening back.

Gradually the bar began to fill up with the Rangers supporters until there was not a seat vacant. We waited for the fireworks.

There were none.

Out of several hundred that crowded into the bar, I saw only a handful that were drinking alcoholic beverages and they caused no problems. Most drank coke and munched quietly on their sandwiches. I would like to say that I was proud of them. Well yes, of course I was, but at the same time I was slightly put out. Over the years I had regaled Barbara, a sophisticated Essex girl (or is that now considered a contradiction in terms?), with tales of Glasgow mayhem and now the chickens had come home to roost. She would never believe my stories again.

CHAPTER 15

Tap Dancing at the Cave Cooperative

The P & O ferries had gone on strike. Or rather, the seamen had, so there were very few sailings and none at all on the Dover–Calais route. There was also trouble on Sealink where the sailors had taken action in sympathy. The general view was that one did not stand a very good chance of getting a ferry to France at this particular moment.

I discussed this with David in the office.

'You are wasting your time,' he said. 'You will spend the whole of Easter sitting on the quay at Dover.'

'Perhaps,' I replied, 'but I am going to book up with Sealink and give it a go.'

We decided that the thing to do was to go for an early ferry so that if that one was cancelled there might be other opportunities later on. We booked on the 7.30 am Sealink ferry.

Normally we arrive at the ferry port about an hour before departure. On this occasion we must have felt that getting there early would be an advantage because we arrived there at ten minutes to six.

The man in the little box checked our tickets and waved us through. After passport control another official checked our tickets.

'Go straight on board,' he said.

Normally we have a car to follow. This time we were the pathfinders but we soon found our way on board a Sealink ferry. We counted four other cars ahead of us. As soon as we had parked the doors behind us were closed and the ship made ready for sea.

The rest of the vehicle deck was filled with trailers. There were no cabs in front of the trailers so there were no drivers.

When we got upstairs we discovered that it was one of the big new Sealink ferries. It certainly seemed to be very roomy but this could have been due to the complete absence of passengers.

When we got to the cafeteria in search of breakfast we did discover the other passengers – all seven of them.

The cafeteria staff had obviously expected a few more people judging by the amount of food spread out before us. They entreated us to have an extra egg, another slice of fried bread, just a few more mushrooms. I obliged to the best of my ability.

We were in the English Channel by 6 a.m. I approved of this form of travelling and made a mental note to try arrange all future journeys during strike actions.

During our absence from St. Crispin the village had been binned.

When we first bought our house in the village we had seen the other villagers hang up carrier bags of rubbish each evening. These were collected early the following morning. We were very impressed with this seven days a week refuse collection service from outside your own front door.

The refuse collection man who drove the tractor around the village was Monsieur Lagarde's son-in-law. He was one of the first people we met in the village. He was always eager to have a chat with us and help us out with any problems.

My first thought on seeing that the village had been converted to bins was that Monsieur Lagarde's son-in-law might be out of a job.

My second thought was that I had just bought a new hook for my rubbish. After the last night of the *fête* the previous September I had gone out to hang up my rubbish only to discover that my hook had disappeared. Monsieur Lagarde had observed me trying to hang my carrier bag on a non-existent hook and told me that this sort of thing is not uncommon.

'The *fête* attracts many hooligans,' he said, 'and they do things like stealing hooks from walls.'

I had determined that there would not be a repeat of this performance the following year. I visited the local hardware shop and selected a large steel hook.

Monsieur Lagarde nodded approval as he watched me drill some holes in the wall and secure the hook with several large screws. Unless they carried a screwdriver the hooligans would not be able to pinch this hook.

I now found myself with a gleaming metal hook that served no purpose whatsoever.

The old refuse disposal system had been relatively quiet. There was the noise of the tractor but depositing the carrier bags in the trailer did not make any noise and Monsieur Lagarde's son-in-law, being of sound mind, did not shout to himself during the exercise. It also took place at the fairly reasonable hour of seven in the morning.

The new bin men come, in an enormous vehicle, three times a week at between two and three in the morning. The noise is incredible as they wheel the bins into range of the mechanical arms that lift them into the air and upend them into the back of the lorry. Just to avoid any possibility of a moment of silence the bin men continually shout to each other.

Still one must not stand in the way of progress and after all it is only noise.

As it turned out Monsieur Lagarde's son-in-law was not out of a job. He appeared to be the local council odd-job man. We saw him doing jobs like sweeping up the dogs droppings, of which there were a considerable number, and cleaning out the village fountain. He seemed to be very contented in his work.

Considering the number of dogs in the village I did not think that he would ever be out of a job. French village dogs run loose unless they are vicious guard dogs in which case they are chained up. I have never seen a dog on a lead in the village.

My favourite dog is Rusti. He belongs to the *café* and is generally to be found lying under one of the tables. I cannot say whether he is a thoroughbred or not but there is certainly a large amount of Briard (the French equivalent of an Old English Sheepdog) in him. He has a thick black coat that gives the indication of never having been combed. He really is incredibly scruffy in a pleasant sort of way. We offer him our spare cubes of sugar when we have our *café cognacs*. He will amble slowly over and relieve us of them then return to his spot to get on with the important business of taking things easy.

His lack of activity gives the impression that he is quite old but on one occasion I saw him spring into action like a two year old.

I was leaning over the terrace railing enjoying the tranquillity of life in the village square when there was a sudden surge of activity. A dog was being chased by what looked like a bundle of dirty old rags. As they got closer I could see that the bundle of rags was Rusti. I wondered what the other dog had done to Rusti to upset him sufficiently for this level of exertion.

Just along the square from my tree is another tree where one of the village ladies has spent a lot of time planting flowers round the base. It was here that Rusti caught the other dog. As I observed the ensuing action I realised that the other dog was in fact a bitch and it became very clear why Rusti had been chasing her. The poor lady's flowers suffered quite a bit as Rusti had his evil way.

I liked Rusti even more after that. He is not really old and infirm. He is just conserving his energies for the important things in life.

The other dog I like is a brown and white dog of unknown breed. I have often seen him wandering round the village but it was the episode with the travelling greengrocer that endeared him to me.

Mobile shops come to the village all the time. You can have an excellent choice of cheese, meat, fish, *charcuterie,* fruit and vegetables without having to leave the village. You can also buy clothes and shoes on some days.

The old ladies spend a lot of money at the mobile shops. I suppose they are buying for large families but I always feel a bit self-conscious when I compare my paltry purchases with theirs.

I remember the first time I went to the mobile butchers in the square. All I wanted were some of his excellent sausages to barbecue. There were about six old ladies in the queue ahead of me. They all bought the most expensive cuts of meat in considerable quantity. They all also bought sausages by the metre. As I got nearer the front of the queue I could sees the amount of sausage in the tub disappearing by the minute. Soon there was only one metre of sausage left and there was still a lady in front of me. It was Madame Garcia. I did consider reminding her that I had been instrumental in providing her with transport in the shape of a nice new bicycle and asking her to lay off the sausage. Instead I decided to let fate take its course. She took the sausage.

I am happy to report that the butcher produced another tub containing about fifty metres of sausage so all was well.

TAP DANCING AT THE CAVE COOPERATIVE

Madame Garcia was also there at the greengrocer episode.

I had made my selection of three tomatoes and a lettuce and was waiting in the queue. The ladies were all chatting away to each other and quite successfully jumping the queue ahead of me. This was a pretty pointless exercise for them as they did not go away after making their purchases. They hung around and chatted.

Suddenly there was a great commotion amongst the ladies and shrieks of *'Michel, regardez!'*

I followed their pointed fingers and there was my second favourite village dog. There was a large bunch of leeks tied together leaning against the stone surround of one of the trees in the village square. The dog had wandered over to the leeks, cocked his leg and relieved himself all over them.

Michel did not bat an eyelid. He picked up the leeks, walked over to the fountain, doused them a couple of times in the water, and returned them to their original spot. He did not even kick the dog. The ladies nodded their approval of his actions but I noticed that none of them bought leeks that day. No doubt the next village thought that they were the best leeks that they had ever tasted.

Sunday is the day to avoid the *boulangerie* if you are at all pressed for time. Easter Sunday is the worst Sunday of all.

It is not just the old ladies but the whole population of the village that squeezes into the shop.

On Easter Sunday there are two people serving but progress is still very slow because everybody is buying *pâtisserie*. If you buy *pâtisserie*, even a single small tart, it is put in a box, wrapped in pretty paper and a piece of ribbon tied round it.

On a normal Sunday there are always some nice tarts available but never a great deal of choice. On Easter Sunday the shelves are crammed with a wide variety of cakes and tarts and *brioches* and strange looking loaves. Making a selection is not something that should be rushed.

It has taken us a long time to come to terms with the cost of *pâtisserie* in France. The old ladies think nothing of paying seventy or eighty francs for a tart. Now we do the same, not every Sunday like the rest of the village, but at least occasionally. Of late it has become more frequent because, as Mr. Kipling would say, they are exceedingly good tarts.

Coteaux de Languedoc wines are very good. Although the area has, in the past, been known for the high volume production of common wines, today the vintners are returning to their old traditions of producing high quality wines. The old traditions date back to the Roman occupation and the Languedoc houses, almost certainly, the oldest vineyard in France. I picked up a leaflet that gave me some information on the wines of the Languedoc. This told me that Cicero in *Pro Fonteio* sings the praises of the wines of this area. I also read that in 1830 Presidents Monroe and Jefferson of the United States were regular consumers of the wines of St-Georges-d'Orques, near Montpellier. I am not convinced of the wisdom of using Presidents of the United States to promote fine wines, based upon the recent incumbents of the office. Peanuts or jelly beans, yes; wines, definitely not. I also note that President Monroe died in 1831 which I am sure had nothing to do with his liking for the wines of St-Georges-d'Orques. Even stranger is the fact that President Jefferson died in 1826 which does bring into question his ability to judge the quality of wines in 1830. However I am sure that few people reading the wine pamphlet are aware of these facts and I certainly was not before referring to my encyclopedia.

We needed some wine so we went to our favourite *Cave Cooperative*. There are two villages in the immediate area that are recognised as producing good quality red wine. They are both pretty drinkable but we selected this *Cave Cooperative* because it also does a very good *vin mousseux* called *Les Deux Vierges*. It is ideal for the *kir royal* and is also good enough to be served on its own. We promised a friend twelve virgins for his birthday and delivered them in the shape of a box of six bottles. He was not too disappointed after he sampled the wine.

The *Cave Cooperative* also sell their most popular red wine in large bottles. We buy the 5 litre size quite frequently because they are handy to give people as presents. The wine is good and it is quite a novelty for the guests of the recipient when he produces this large bottle at a dinner party.

On one occasion the Cooperative had run out of 5 litre bottles and I had to go for the larger 12 litre size. We opened the bottle on a nice summer's day at home when we were having some friends round for a buffet lunch. Normally a 5 litre bottle plus a few smaller bottles of red were quite sufficient for this annual event. We was convinced that a lot of the 12 litre bottle would have to be thrown away but, nothing of the sort. They polished off the lot and we still had to open a couple more small bottles! This is the problem with buying wine in large containers. Once it is open the capacity of the guests will always expand to match the supply of the wine.

There were quite a few people waiting in the *vente directe* area of the *Cave Cooperative*. It was a large room with pumps, like petrol pumps, at one end where the containers are filled up.

It always takes a while to be served as everything is done in sequence. One transaction cannot overlap another. If the customer ahead of you has a couple of forty litre containers to be filled there is no question of you being served while the filling is taking place. After the containers have been filled and the money handed over a large form has to be filled in. This all takes time.

One must just accept this, relax and observe one's fellow customers.

A young couple were immediately in front of us in the queue. Each carried a large empty container. The chap was in a lively mood and broke into a sort of tap dance routine on the tiled floor. His companion told him to stop acting the fool. He continued to horse around. She told him that it would be all right to do that sort of thing if he was any good at it but he was just making a fool of himself. He said, ' You show me how to do it then.'

She did. She did an excellent little tap dance routine and earned a round of applause from the watchers when she finished. From the look on her chap's face it was obvious that this was the first he knew of her skills as a dancer.

Then there was the old lady sitting at the table sampling a glass of red wine. She was clearly enjoying herself and the dance routine probably made her day. She was the passenger from the taxi parked outside. The taxi driver was busy buying wine. He bought four cases and loaded them into the boot of the taxi. Had the old lady called a taxi to go and collect her wine? Or had the taxi driver stopped to collect some wine for himself and parked his customer at the table while he did so?

It is never boring waiting in the queue at the *Cave Cooperative* if you bother to observe the other customers.

Just along the road from the *Cave Cooperative* is a nice restaurant with a parrot and a dog. The dog is a Newfoundland and if you happen to be passing through the village on a hot summer's day have a look in the fountain. You will see the Newfoundland totally immersed except for its head and its tail which sticks straight up in the air. For some reason it does not want to get its tail wet.

The parrot has a perch on a tree outside the restaurant. From time to time the parrot will become a bit excited and start screeching. When this happens the cook comes out and throws a glass of water over it. If you happen to be sitting on the other side of the parrot that is just too bad.

It was time for stage two of the terrace to begin. There was a loft ladder from the top floor up to a trap door on the roof terrace. We wanted to replace the loft ladder with a spiral staircase. A small 'house' would have to be built on the terrace before I would be able to install the spiral staircase.

I drew a plan of the proposed structure. It was not all that small really because we wanted enough room for both a small fridge and for storage of the terrace furniture during the winter. We also wanted to be able to sit inside the little house if the weather was not too good.

Should we ask for planning permission? We decided against it as we wanted to start work straight away. However, as we were not going to seek planning permission, we intended to keep the height of the structure to a minimum.

For financial reasons we would not be employing a builder. I had done some bricklaying at home, for the same reasons, and although my efforts had not been a complete success I had learned quite a lot from the experience. Bricklaying appears to be very easy but the amateur should check regularly that the wall he is building is, in fact, vertical. I became over confident and discovered that I strayed off the straight and narrow. I had a choice of knocking the wall down and starting again or trying to correct my error. I chose the latter option. The end result was safe enough but not too impressive to the experienced eye. The problem was easily solved by some fast growing ivy.

I mapped out the area for the structure on the roof and went off to buy some bricks and cement. The bricks are referred to as *rouges*. They come in all shapes and sizes. Some are only about an inch thick but internal walls are built using these bricks. I found this out to my cost when drilling a hole in one of our internal walls. Barbara was papering the wall in the next room when three inches of masonry drill suddenly appeared through the section that she had just papered.

The cement is called *plâtre de briquetage* and it is wonderful stuff. It is sort of like sticky porridge and it makes laying the bricks very easy. As all the walls are rendered afterwards you do not need to exercise any great care when laying the bricks other than keeping them in line. This makes bricklaying a speedy business in France, even for the amateur.

When we left the village to return home, my little house was about a metre high and already visible from the far end of the square. Had I made a mistake in not seeking planning permission? Would someone in the village put in a complaint? I would have to wait and see.

CHAPTER 16

The Vice-Presidential Mansion

It was hot in St. Crispin in mid-June that year.

I would have appreciated cooler weather as my major project was to finish the little house on the terrace. There was no shelter up there so I would get up early in the morning and work for about three hours, then pack it in until early evening. The problem was that I had to mix the *plâtre de briquetage* in small quantities because it dried so quickly.

The *maison de toit terrasse* gradually took shape. I had been a bit daring and gone a level of bricks higher than I had originally planned but I still had to duck down when I went inside.

The window and the door had been fitted and now it was time to start on the roof. I used the *tuiles romanes*, the traditional half-round roof tiles that are to be found on most of the village houses. What I did not realise was how heavy they were and how many you need to cover a relatively small space. The tiles had to be carried up three flights of stairs and up a loft ladder. Barbara has never forgotten this experience. She had volunteered to act as builder's mate.

I had used pretty substantial wooden beams to support the roof tiles but as I discovered when the tiles were all in place, they were not quite substantial enough. The door that opened inwards now no longer opened all the way because a beam was in the way.

I decided that this was no great problem. I simply cut a bit out of the beam.

The following morning I had the same problem. The beam had bent a little more under the weight of the tiles. I could not continue to cut bits out of the beam so I decided to put a metal support across the beams but first I would have to find a way of pushing the beams back to their original position as I had no intention of removing all the tiles.

In the end it was quite simple. I got two stout pieces of wood. I put one piece across the beams and supported it there with the other piece. I then got the jack out of the car and jacked the roof up to the position required and fitted the cross beam. The little house was now complete.

At that time I worked for a Vice-President called Sid. He was about four feet six inches tall and universally feared because he bit people's legs off. I liked Sid because he added a touch of colour to an otherwise fairly drab organisation and also because he was clever. As Sid was the only person I knew who would be able to walk around my little house without banging his head I decided to name it after him.

Now we always refer to the terrace house as *Sid's House* and there is even a little plaque to record this fact.

As *Sid's House* was now weatherproof, in theory at least, we could start planning for the installation of the spiral staircase.

There is no shortage of places in France to go to buy a spiral staircase. Barbara had seen a shop that specialised in spiral staircases on the outskirts of Montpellier so that was our first port of call.

The staircases were magnificent and so were the prices. They were not DIY models and the cost of the staircase plus the installation would just about have doubled the price of our house.

We tried Castorama which is a big chain of DIY shops in France. They produce a very comprehensive catalogue, of around 500 pages, which has become my Bible. They sell just about everything. If I am considering buying something from another shop I will always consult my Castorama catalogue to compare prices.

We also received another catalogue through the letter box from Kloutou which is fascinating to read. I did not realise the significance of the name until I saw one of their vans. *Louer* means to rent and *tout* means all so the name Kloutou sounds like 'Rent-All' and that is exactly what they do. The range of equipment and machines that their catalogue contains is mind-boggling. My son-in-law, Clive, became quite excited when he was browsing through it. He had discovered a machine that he thought might be able to solve his problem with the moles which kept tunnelling into his garden. This machine was for laying cables. It cuts a trench about three feet deep and about an inch wide in the ground. Clive's idea was that he would cut a trench all the way round his garden and fill it with concrete. The moles, he felt, would soon get fed up with banging their heads on a subterranean concrete wall. So far he has not attempted to implement the plan but if Kloutou ever comes to the UK then he might just give it a try.

Castorama did have some nice wooden spiral staircases but they were still on the expensive side.

We consulted our Lapeyre catalogue. Lapeyre, like Castorama is a nationwide chain but they have a more limited product range. We bought the window and door for *Sid's House* from Lapeyre and had been very pleased with the quality of the goods. The catalogue featured a metal spiral staircase, which came in kit form, for around 6000 francs. This was just what we wanted, but would they be able to get us one in time? We would be leaving for home in a couple of weeks.

Absolutely no problem. We stated our requirements to the sales assistant. He entered them into his terminal, pressed a button and the printer produced an invoice for us and a requisition for the store. I gave him my credit card. He did the necessary and handed me my receipt and the requisition. We drove round to the collection point and handed in the requisition. Within ten minutes we had a complete spiral staircase loaded into the car and we were heading towards St. Crispin.

There is a world of difference between the DIY stores in France and those at home. In France they stock a much wider selection of goods but, more importantly, they always have them in stock - even the more expensive items. The prices in France do tend to be a bit higher but so is the quality. The only item that is expensive, and not nearly as good as the UK equivalent, is paint.

We always import our paint.

The instructions for assembling the spiral staircase told us that we needed a hole a metre square in the roof. The hole for the trap door was less than half this size so a little enlarging was necessary. This was a slight problem as the roof was reinforced concrete about six inches thick.

I had promised Barbara that I would find a way of enlarging the hole that caused the absolute minimum of mess. I thought that if I could cut a reasonably deep groove with an angle grinder then I could give it a bash with a heavy hammer and it would break away. Not a chance. The concrete was much too hard for the angle grinder to make much of an impact so I would have to think of something else. But what?

After a period of serious deliberation, which produced not even a glimmer of an idea, I decided to renegotiate my position with Barbara.

I explained to her that the only way I could think of to enlarge the hole was to get a sledge hammer and have a good bash at it. This, I conceded, could result in a little bit of dust and rubble finding its way into the house but I would put down some plastic sheeting on the landing. Barbara reluctantly acquiesced.

The next stage required some careful planning. The problem was the loft ladder. It was a heavy duty telescopic sort that would have to be removed before I could bash a bigger hole. However, once it was removed and I had enlarged the hole there was no way that it could be used again for access to and from the terrace and we did not own a ladder.

In the end it was fairly simple to work out the required sequence of events.

Barbara and I would assemble the spiral staircase on the landing. I would go up on the roof terrace with my tools, including the sledge hammer, unbolt the loft ladder and lower it to the landing. I would then bash the concrete with a sledge hammer until I had a sufficiently large hole. Barbara and I would manoeuvre the spiral staircase into position and I would fix the top step to the terrace. Once that was done I could climb down the spiral staircase and fix the base to the landing. A piece of cake. What could go wrong?

They really were very well designed these spiral staircases. You only had to fix them in two places and they were as solid as a rock.

Before operations commenced I wandered down into the square as I had seen my neighbour sitting on the bench.

We exchanged *bonjours* and I gave him one of my serious looks.

'*Je vais faire un trou dans le toit de ma maison*.' I said.

He nodded.

'*Avec un grand marteau*,' I continued.

He nodded again.

'*Il y aurait beaucoup de bruit*,' I confessed.

Two nods this time. One of understanding and one of agreement. It would be difficult to make a hole in the roof with a big hammer without making a lot of noise.

'*Peut-être*,' I ventured, '*si votre femme est dans la maison vous lui dites ces choses*.'

'*Non, non*,' he said, '*c'est pas nécessaire. Le bruit n'est pas une probleme*.'

I shrugged. At least I had tried to warn the poor lady. I turned and started walking back to the house when I heard a call of *Monsieur* from behind me. I turned to see my neighbour beckoning me to return.

'*Pourquoi?*' he asked when I faced him once again.

'*Pourquoi,*' I responded.

'*Pourquoi vous faites un trou dans le toit de votre maison?*'

'Ah,' I replied. '*C'est pour un escalier en spiral*.'

He was impressed. This might well be the first *éscalier en spiral* in the village.

In retrospect I was quite pleased that he had called me back otherwise there could have been yet another story going round the village about *les Anglais*. 'They bang holes in their roof, you know.'

We got on well with the villagers. We did not spend a long time chatting to them because our French was really too limited and most of them speak in a *patois* that seems strongly influenced by Catalan or Italian. On the other hand we never missed handing out the *bonjours* to anyone who happened to cross our paths.

Another reason why we were readily accepted, I believe, was because the villagers could see that we did a lot of the work on the house ourselves. Many people buy holiday homes, employ an architect and a builder, and eventually move in without having had any personal contact with the villagers or the *Mairie* whatsoever. We had done it all ourselves and the villagers could see this. Every time I drove into the square after visiting Castorama or Lapeyre there would be a small audience, on the bench outside the *Credit Agricole*, who would inspect my purchases with interest.

I also established myself as a *très sérieux* DIY man when they saw me unload a nine inch angle grinder from the car one day.

Operation Spiral Staircase proceeded according to plan. Well, according to my plan anyway. Barbara took a different view. As soon as

I started to bash the edge of the opening in the roof it became clear that I was going to make a lot of mess. The plastic sheeting I had put down would not exactly contain the deluge. It is not possible, you see, to gently bash your way through a reinforced concrete roof. You have to hit it pretty hard. The rubble went everywhere. Into the bedrooms. Down the stairs into the lounge. There was, of course, also a sizeable pile building up on the landing.

I did not make the hole quite as large as the instructions had suggested. It was about ten centimetres short of the recommended metre when I placed my hammer on the ground and told Barbara it was safe to come out of her temporary air raid shelter. I now had to break the news to her that the rubble would have to be cleared from the landing before the staircase could be put in position and I could not assist in this task as I was on the roof with no way of getting down.

Barbara was very good about it really. She beavered away while I sipped a cold beer and watched the villagers go about their business. Did I mention that we had bought a *Sid-sized* fridge for *Sid's House* ? Even though it was very small it was too large to go through the trap door so like the windows and doors for *Sid's House* it had to be hauled up the outside by a rope. Barbara insisted that all these little exercises took place under cover of darkness as she did not want an audience of villagers watching our strange practices.

The time had arrived. The staircase was pretty heavy, being made of metal, but we gradually edged it into position. But no - it must be out of position because the top step did not reach the side of the hole. But yes - it was in position - I had made the hole too large. It was impossible to fix the staircase. I must confess I panicked. It was not the fact that I was marooned on the roof with no way down. That was bad enough, but presumably Barbara could borrow a ladder from somebody. The problem was that I did not have the faintest idea what to do about the staircase. I could not glue bits of concrete back on to make the hole smaller.

This was a stressful situation. I had bought a house in France to avoid stress. I took a grip of myself and the panic gradually subsided. I must calmly review the situation and devise a plan of action. What was the first step? Of course, I must allocate blame. I could see from Barbara's expression that she had already done so.

SID'S HOUSE
KRONENBOURG
APPELLATION
CÔTEAUX DU
LANGUEDOC
CONTRÔLÉE

I re-read the instructions. There was absolutely no doubt that they said the hole had to be a metre wide. I threw them down to Barbara who read them and grudgingly agreed that it was not entirely my fault. I began to feel better already.

There was only one answer. I would have to find a nice thick piece of wood, about two feet square, that I would attach to the top step and then to the roof. I did not have such a piece of wood about my person nor was there anything like that in the house. A quick visit to *Monsieur Bricolage*, the local DIY store, was called for. I could not possibly send Barbara off on her own as it was unlikely they would have exactly what we wanted and compromises of a DIY nature would have to be made. I would have to get down from the roof.

'Do you know the French for ladder?' I shouted down to Barbara.

'No,' she said, in a tentative voice that indicated that she suspected what was coming next.

'It is *échelle*,' I said. 'Could you just pop out into the square and ask somebody if you can borrow their *échelle*.'

'Certainly not,' Barbara said. 'They already think that we are mad. I am not going to let them know that my husband has got himself stranded on the roof of his own house. You can jump down.'

In the end, and with great difficulty, Barbara managed to steady the spiral staircase in a sufficiently upright position for me to scramble down.

Monsieur Bricolage came up with the goods. The new approach to installation was a bit more difficult than the original concept but we managed it.

The moment of stress and panic had passed. It must have left its mark however because when Taff called round that evening he commented that I was not looking my usual calm and cheerful self.

The spiral staircase was a great success and completely steady even after Taff, who is no lightweight, had been up and down a few times.

CHAPTER 17

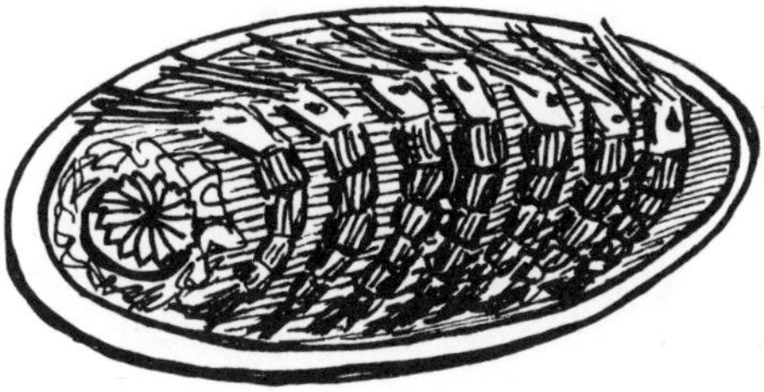

To Gain a Chariot but Lose a Crown

The Vieux Logis had definitely closed down. There are lots of other good restaurants in the area but not one that could produce a *pintade aux champignons* quite like the Vieux Logis.

We now settled on Chez Isabelle as our local Villemarché restaurant. It is open all year round and well patronised by the locals. The food is simple but of a consistently high standard. The menu never changes and we have got into a dreadful rut there. We always start with a *kir* and a *pastis*, courtesy of the house if Isabelle is in attendance. Next we have a bottle of *Listel Gris de Gris* and either share a *pizza fruits de mer* between us or have some *moules farcies*. The pizzas are to be highly recommended. They have a thin crisp base and are about the size of dust bin lids. Our main course is usually the *gambas à la persillade* which are large prawns grilled with lots of garlic. These are not cheap but you get a very generous helping. We used occasionally to have to leave one or two until our elder daughter introduced the American doggy-bag system. She had seen a sign outside a restaurant in Marseillan and asked Barbara what it meant.

'*Plats à emporter*,' Barbara said. 'That means they do take-aways.'

The next time Vikki went to Chez Isabelle and she could not finish her *gambas* she simply pointed to the remaining ones and said, '*Pour emporter, s'il vous plaît*.' This was no problem. They gave her them on a plate covered in foil.

Chez Isabelle do excellent *haricot verts* and *frites*. We normally have *frites* with our prawns as we could then eat our main course entirely without the aid of cutlery. The first time we went there we ordered two lots of *frites*. Up came this enormous platter of *frites* which we could not possibly finish. The next time we ordered a single portion. Up came exactly the same size of platter. This time we stopped thinking of our waist measurement and polished off the lot - after all, it was only a single portion.

The new Villemarché bypass has been finished. This has made a big difference to the town as heavy lorries no longer trundle through the main street one after another. A couple of new restaurants have opened. One is Chinese and we thought we should give it our support as starting a Chinese restaurant in a small town like Villemarché cannot be an entirely risk-free enterprise. The food was very good but it was quite hard work trying to communicate in French with the Chinese waiter in an attempt to find out what the various dishes were. We foolishly thought, being fairly familiar with Chinese food at home, that we would recognise some of the dishes on the menu. This was not the case and we ended up ordering absolutely blind. It was an interesting experience but one which we have not repeated.

The other new restaurant is French. The first time we tried it they forgot our second course and the meal deteriorated into a bit of a farce. On top of that I was violently ill in the middle of the night. Being of a generous and forgiving nature I decided to give them a second chance. Once again I was ill during the night so we have scored that one off our list.

There was a Mas up in the hills that we also liked to visit in good weather where you could eat outside in the spacious, if somewhat wild, garden. They put their wood-burning bread oven on at weekends and as a starter we would have one of their small deep pizza's which were absolutely delicious. When we first went there Barbara noticed that a small boy, who was probably just over a year old, had got himself on to a chair and was having difficulty getting down. I must confess that I had also noticed this. I suppose that this illustrates the difference between Barbara, who is a very practical person, and myself. I thought that little boy is going to fall off that chair. Barbara went over and helped him down.

It was at the Mas that we learned an important lesson. We had been looking forward to going there for some time and had finally made it only to find that it had been booked for a wedding party. We returned a couple of days later to find out that we had chosen the evening that they were closed. We told them that this was the second time that we had been disappointed. The *Patron* apologised and said that if we would like to eat the same humble fare that he was offering his *pension* guests then we were quite welcome to join them. It is just a hot *chèvre* salad to start with, followed by *moules* and *frites*. We readily accepted. He kept bringing plates of *moules* and *frites* until we could eat no more. We declined the cheese and he said that all he could offer us for dessert was *banane flambée au cognac*. The whole meal was delicious and including the wine and coffee came to about a hundred and fifty francs for the two of us. The lesson is that it is usually a good idea to book into an hotel on the evening that the restaurant is closed to the public. The service is always good as there are not too many diners and, in our experience, they always produce a very good meal for their guests.

When we first went shopping in Villemarché there was only one supermarket. It was called Codec in those days but a couple of years ago the name was changed to Lion. About the same time a new Intermarché was built on the edge of the bypass and they seem to get most of the trade these days.

Car parking at Intermarché is a bit of a shambles as everyone ignores the lines and parks where he likes. One day they decided to do something about this.

We had chosen to shop at Intermarché that day and, in true French fashion, I parked illegally. When I went to get a trolley, or *chariot* as the French call them, I discovered that I did not have the necessary ten franc piece. I went to one of the check-out girls and asked her to change a twenty franc note. She told me that she was not allowed to give change but the lady in the bakery would probably help me out.

The bakery is part of the supermarket but you pay separately. I explained my predicament to the bakery lady who said she was very sorry but she did not have much change. Why didn't I try the checkouts? I pleaded with *Madame la Boulangerie* but to no avail. She would not change my 20 franc note. Then she decided to take pity on me. She said that she would lend me a ten franc piece. I thought this was a very generous gesture as she did not know me from Adam. She also must have been thinking the same because she asked for my car keys as colateral. I happily handed them over as I was anxious to start the shopping.

It was when we were right down at the far end of the supermarket that we heard something familiar in the announcement coming over the loudspeaker. It was our car registration number. What had happened? Had someone crashed into it? I hurried to the checkouts.

A very officious looking man was waiting for me.

'*C'est votre voiture?*' he enquired.

I admitted that the car in question belonged to me.

'You have parked in a *zone interdit*,' he informed me in stern tones. 'You must move the car at once.'

I apologised and said that if he would just give me a few minutes to finish my shopping I would remove the car from the *zone interdit*. This was a bit of an exaggeration judging by the length of the queues at the checkouts but it made no difference anyway.

He pulled himself up another inch and folded his arms.

'This situation is *très sérieux*,' he advised me. It was necessary that I moved the car immediately.

'That is not possible,' I replied.

He grew a little redder in the face and demanded to know why it was not possible.

I informed him that the reason why I could not move the car was because I did not have the car key.

'Your wife has the car key?' he enquired.

'No.'

'Who has the car key?'

I told him, with a perfectly straight face that the bakery lady had the key to my car.

He turned and looked across at the bakery lady.

'She has your car key?'

'Yes'.

'*Pourquoi?*'

'Because I owe her ten francs' I explained.

'Then give her ten frances.'

'That is not possible'

'*Pourquoi?*'

'Because the ten francs is in the *chariot.*'

This was too much for him. He went over to verify my story with the bakery lady. The discussion became a little heated but in the end she handed him the keys which he presented to me.

'*Immédiatement*,' he said.

I moved the car and rejoined Barbara to continue the shopping. When we had finished and loaded the purchases into the car I went over to the bakery to return the ten francs. Although we were not in need of any bread I felt that I should buy something to show goodwill. I saw a small brown loaf that looked a bit like a wholemeal baguette. I bought it, thanked Madame profusely for the loan, and returned to the car.

'Why did you buy a loaf?' Barbara asked me. 'We have plenty of bread at home.'

That evening, in view of Barbara's comment, I felt obliged to try the small brown loaf. I took one bite and felt a crunch. It was incredibly hard bread and there, stuck to the piece that I removed from my mouth was an expensive crown from one of my front teeth.

This was the beginning of that holiday so I had to go around gap-toothed for a couple of weeks. I was not too worried about my appearance, it was the fact that I lisped when I spoke that upset me. Had I been in Spain rather than France I would have spoken the language with a quite passable accent.

We would often forsake the autoroutes and travel back on the *route nationale*. After Lodève the road begins to wind steeply upwards past the Pas de L'Escalette where the road used to end many years ago. In those days the travellers had to climb up ladders to the plateau above, the Causse de Larzac, where another coach would be waiting for them to continue on their journey.

The scenery is quite spectacular as one ascends, and no less so when eventually the road winds down to the bustling town of Millau. It was close to Millau that we stayed in an hotel on our original voyage of discovery. I will always remember their *melon au porto*. Their approach was very simple. They took a complete melon, cut a small piece off the top, and scooped out the seeds. However large the capacity of the melon it was filled with neat port. That year the melons were very big and we were very contented diners although the following day it was difficult to remember what we had actually eaten.

We are creatures of habit. When we go home by the *route nationale* we always stop at the Viaduct de Garabit for lunch. This railway bridge was built by none other than Monsieur Eiffel of Parisian tower fame. Lunch consists of *baguettes* filled with smoked salmon and washed down with a very cold *Picpoul de Pinet*. There is an ideal spot for parking as the road ascends towards St. Flour and you can look down on the lake below as you enjoy your little snack.

You can now join the autoroute south of Clèrmont Ferrand but when we started using this route you had to continue on the *route nationale* through Moulins and Nevers and join the autoroute north of Montargis.

Normally we would stay overnight around La Charité-sur-Loire and it was when we were heading towards La Charité, from an unusual direction that we discovered the chateau owned by a lady who had once been a deckhand on a fishing boat out of Sète. I do not know whether it was a *thonier* or a *chalutier* as it was after I had spoken to her that I did my research on the subject.

We had spent ages searching for a particular hotel, out in the wilds, and when we had eventually discovered it, we found that it was *complet*. We started across country towards La Charité and, in a small village on the banks of the Loire, we came across what looked like a very pleasant little restaurant. They had no accommodation but the chateau at the other end of the village could perhaps accommodate us. Normally we would have ignored this advice as we did not frequent chateau hotels. They tend to be well beyond our pocket. However, it was getting late and we were tired.

It was not a very large chateau but it was certainly a chateau. We had some difficulty finding any sign of human life but there was animal life in abundance. Eventually a lady in her early thirties appeared. We conversed in French for a few sentences and I established that they did have a room for us. She then switched to English which she spoke with an American accent and asked us if we would like to see the room.

It was a very attractive room with large windows giving a magnificent view of the Loire across a few hundred yards of garden. The private *salle de bains* was also of a very generous size. I began to get a little apprehensive about the price.

'Did you see us advertised in the guide?' she asked. I told her that had discovered her chateau entirely by chance.

TO GAIN A CHARIOT BUT LOSE A CROWN

'Ah, well, you will not know the price. It is 250 francs including breakfast. Is that OK?'

I said that was OK. The view alone made the room worth double.

When I went to get our things out of the car I was accompanied by one of the many dogs, a large Alsatian. As soon as I opened the boot it stuck its nose in and investigated all our belongings. I waited until it was completely satisfied as I did not want to upset it by slamming the lid on its head.

The chateau was not in a wonderful state of repair and the grounds were not what one would call well groomed. It was, however, a charming spot. There was a donkey wandering around and some goats in a pen. There were also expensive children's toys, mostly broken, scattered around the grounds.

We met Madame's young son but there was no sign of her husband. She recommended the restaurant we had visited so that was where we had our meal before collapsing exhausted into our bed.

The breakfast was the best that I have had in any hotel in France. Madame could not be precise about when she would bring breakfast to our room. It depended on when the baker made his delivery but it would be between eight and nine.

When it arrived it was straight out of the oven. There were *croissants* and *pain au chocolat*. There were currant buns and apple turnovers. There were also lots of good coffee, fruit juices and a large basket of fresh fruit. It was a beautiful sunny morning so we sat by the open windows looking at the Loire and munching happily. All this for 250 francs.

We paid Madame and promised that we would return soon.

It was, in fact, over a year later when we called at the chateau again. We had not booked but thought that we would try our luck. I had never really found out how many rooms were available to let but I suspect that it was no more than two or three.

Madame was easier to find the second time. Yes, she could let us have a room but, wait a moment, had we not stayed in her house before?

We admitted that we had and apologised for the fact that we had taken so long to make a return visit.

'This is wonderful, she cried. 'Put your things in your room and come and join me on the terrace for some champagne.'

It was a hot summer's day and the prospect of a nice glass of cold champagne sounded like a very good idea to us.

There seemed to be as many dogs running around as ever. The little dog which accompanied us to our room was not one that we had encountered last time and there was no sign of the Alsatian. We were in the same room as before and we were pleased to see, when we looked out the window, that the donkey and the goats were still keeping the grass at a reasonable level in the rear garden.

It was while we sitting sipping champagne that Madame mentioned her career as a fisherwoman.

We had told her where our house was situated.

'Ah, that is not too far from Sète,' she said. 'Do you ever go there?'

'Not very often,' I admitted. 'It gets very crowded in the summer and they steal your spare wheels in winter.'

We were conducting the conversation in English and 'spare wheel' was not a term that she was familiar with. I proudly displayed my limited knowledge of French by saying, '*On a volé ma roue de secours à Sète*.'

She told us how she had worked as deck hand on one of the large fishing boats that you can watch manoeuvring in the narrow channel as you sit at one of the quayside restaurants.

'I am the only woman crew member to have worked on these boats,' she stated proudly.

We met one of her stepsons who was almost as old as she was, and also another gentleman, a little older, who popped in for a quick drink and to say that he was *desolé* that he could not stay overnight on this visit.

There was still no sign of her husband.

The breakfast was as good as ever and the price was still 250 francs. This time we had also had champagne on the terrace. It was extremely pleasant but I could not see how Madame stood much chance of making any profit out of the enterprise. Next time, I resolved, I would at least provide the champagne.

CHAPTER 18

Chapeau Melon et Bottes de Cuir

In all my years in the company I had never been on a business trip to Montpellier and now, suddenly, one had come up. I was accompanied by Fred, the reluctant engineering convert to marketing. Fred and I are good friends and the one thing that marketing and engineering do agree on is that most problems can be solved over a glass of something.

Neither of us were familiar with Montpellier. I had stayed at an hotel there many years before but could not really remember anything about the place. My more recent experiences had involved getting lost when trying to drive through.

David knew Montpellier well, and he gave us directions to an area where we would find some good restaurants. We strolled out from the hotel with every intention of taking his advice. The problem was that it began to rain quite heavily. It was warm rain so we were not to concerned but after a while the puddles began to get deeper.

Fred turned to me with a pained expression on his face.

'Blow this for a game of soldiers,' he said. 'I've got a hole in my shoe.'

He held up his foot and sure enough there was a sizeable hole to be seen.

'That's strange,' I said. 'I've also got a hole in my shoe.' This was a true statement and I showed him the evidence. Here we were, two middle managers in a large multi-national company, and we were having to seek shelter because we had holes in our shoes. Had we had some training in economics, no doubt we would have viewed this incident as an omen of the recession that was about to engulf us.

We sought shelter in the nearest doorway. It happened to be an Indian restaurant. The smell wafting out was quite appetizing. The thing that clinched it was the reaction that we would get from David when we told him that we had followed his directions and ended up eating in an Indian restaurant. He would be horrified.

I have eaten in Indian restaurants in Paris and it was not an experience that I particularly wanted to repeat. The food in the restaurant in Montpellier was very different from an 'English' Indian restaurant but still very good in its own way. David, as we expected, thought that we were a couple of Philistines when we told him how valuable his directions had been.

Unfortunately we had to devote our time in Montpellier to business matters so we did not get the opportunity to spend any time in St. Crispin.

Montpellier seems to be a very pleasant town and the inhabitants are very friendly and relaxed. As I stood in the large egg-shaped Place de la Comédie on the sunny morning following the rainy evening, there was a man practising with a large boomerang. The Place was quite crowded but nobody seemed concerned. I watched for a while but he was obviously proficient because he never had to move more than a couple of steps to catch the returning missile. There did not seem to be any imminent chance of bloodshed so I got bored and moved on.

As Barbara and I drove through Montpellier one Sunday morning on our way to the autoroute we came upon a substantial *bouchon*. This came as a surprise on a Sunday but soon we saw the reason. There was an enormous boot sale in progress just on the outskirts of the town. It looked well worth a visit. When I'm able to spend more time in France I will give Montpellier the attention that it deserves.

The Mediterranean is half an hour from our village. It is a pleasant drive although the scenery going in that direction mainly consists of mile after mile of vineyards. It is a reassuring sight to the wine lover but does become a bit boring after a while. In the other direction you quickly reach the hills and river gorges and the scenery is quite spectacular.

We made the trip to the beach perhaps once or twice a week as Barbara likes to swim in the sea. There is a long stretch of sandy beach

RESTAURANT
INDIENNE
TAJ MAHAL
PLATS A
EMPORTER

between Marseillan Plage and Sète which never gets very crowded. It is also a very respectable family beach. Most women sunbathe topless but that is as far as they go. Some of the beaches in the area are for more specialist tastes I am told. This information was supplied to me by a particular party who keeps discovering these places, he claims, purely by accident.

There was one occasion when a couple in their late twenties rushed on to the beach, took off all their clothes, had a quick swim, dressed again and rushed off. The tourists found this quite amusing. It was the French families, mostly locals, who took great exception to this outrageous behaviour.

There are times, however, when I feel that topless sunbathing can be a little embarrassing. I almost had such an experience when Barbara and I were in Nice. The seminar had finished at lunchtime on the third day and most people had immediately left for the airport. As we were planning a touring holiday we thought that we would have a last lie in the sun on the hotel's incredibly small private beach, before a leisurely drive along the coast to our next stopping-off point. As soon as we set foot on the sand I noticed that one of my English colleagues and his wife were already soaking up the sun's rays. She had decided to sunbathe topless which was something that she had not done the previous two days. Fortunately they had not seen us so we had a choice. I took the decision that we should beat a hasty retreat as I was not at all sure of the correct protocol in such a situation. I mean what does one say? If she had suddenly turned up with a new hairdo one would have felt bound to make some complimentary remarks but 'Hello Mary, nice knockers' did not seem to be wholly appropriate.

Just along the coast from Marseillan Plage is Cap d'Agde, famous, amongst other things, for its nudist village. This was featured on a holiday programme on British television a couple of year's ago. You were shown the unclothed *villagers* enjoying themselves at various sporting activities, relaxing in the sun and shopping in the village supermarket. A friend of ours, in the UK, was most surprised to see the familiar figure of his business partner, whom he had no idea went in for such holidays, bending over the frozen food cabinet. I did consider asking him how he recognised his partner if he was bending over at the time but I decided against it.

My favourite story of Cap d'Agde is the one that Taff was told by a couple who had decided to cast off their garments and have a look round the village. They were in a clothes boutique when a couple of very attractive young ladies came in. Naturally the young ladies were not wearing anything. One of them found a dress that took her fancy. She turned to the shop assistant. 'Where is the changing room?'

We went more frequently to the beach when Charlotte, our granddaughter was visiting us. We would take the cool box with us and have a simple lunch of bread and cheese and *pâté*, washed down with nice cold beer, except for Charlotte, who favoured the much more expensive Orangina. We would quit the beach about mid-afternoon to have ice creams at one of the harbour-side *café* restaurants in Mèze.

Mèze is a fishing port on the *Bassin de Thau* famous for *coquillages*. The *Bassin* is a salt water lake that has been created for the cultivation of edible shellfish; chiefly mussels and oysters. The technical term for this is *conchyliculture*. They manage to grow these shellfish quicker in the *Bassin* than in other areas and it is now the major source of supply for Mediterranean France. As you drive into the town you will pass lots of *coquillage* stalls, and naturally all the restaurants are very seafood oriented. We usually have lunch in Mèze at least once when we are in France. There is a restaurant on the harbour that does an excellent sixty franc menu including wine. The last time we went there was on May Day. That is a mistake unless you want to spend the whole day there as there is a big *fête* with lots of floats and entertainment and it is almost impossible to get out once you are in the harbour area.

It was on one of these journeys from Marseillan to Mèze that my daughter informed me that the car was making strange sounds.

'I know that noise,' Barbara cried. 'Stop the car.'

I stopped at a convenient spot and Barbara got out and walked to the back of the car.

'I thought so,' she said.

As I joined her I could see that the empty cradle for the spare wheel was dragging on the ground. They had done it to me again. They had taken my *roue de secours*. This time they had done it in broad daylight in an area where they must have been observed by loads of passing cars.

I like the French. How can you not like a people who have given their highest artistic honour to Sylvester Stallone and given the world the opening ceremony of the 1992 Winter Olympics. Just in case you missed the opening ceremony let me explain. Each country's contingent was led round by a young lady encased in a transparent plastic sphere. Her head and legs stuck out. As she walked along she used her arms to stimulate imitation snowflakes in the sphere. This gave the same effect as the little water-filled glass balls you buy with Father Christmas inside, which, when shaken gives the impression that it is snowing. This was bad enough but, in addition, there was a four line poem narrated for each country. Possibly the poems were not too bad when in the original French but when translated to English for broadcasting to the world they were hilarious. In all honesty I cannot remember any of them but a fictitious example, in the same *genre*, would be:

And now the proud people of Ruritania are here
To win lots of medals it is clear
We wish them luck but what a shame
They have only one contestant with which to make a name

There have been times, however, when I must admit that I have felt that the French have exercised just the slightest hint of selfishness.

We were travelling home by our usual route. We headed towards Montpellier to join the Autoroute Languedocienne. At one point, on a very busy road, you pass over a level crossing. This is not a level crossing as we know it. It crosses a narrow gauge railway that has not been used in living memory. Something had gone wrong and the gates were down.

Where there was a lorry with a driver and a mate, the mate would get out and lift up the gate for the lorry to pass through. Where there was a vehicle with a single occupant the traffic would grind to a halt. The drivers would lean on their horns but they would not do anything constructive to solve the problem.

I was about ten cars from the barrier.

'You drive,' I said to Barbara. 'I am going to go and hold up the barrier.'

With that I leapt out of the car and ran to the railway line. It was remarkably easy to lift the barrier and the traffic began to flow.

When Barbara drove past I noticed that the following three cars had only a single occupant so I let them through as well.

Barbara stopped the car so that I could run along and rejoin her. The three cars that I had kindly let through the barrier all leant on their horns because she was holding them up. The French, I think, have the shortest memories of any nation in the world.

I also quite like French television. It is partly due to the fact there is a fifty-fifty chance that the attractive young woman on the screen will take off her clothes whether you happen to be watching a film, a documentary, or an advertisement. I have not actually seen this happen on the news yet but no doubt one day I will.

Watching, or rather listening to, the television helps to improve my French. This is particularly true of imported films that are dubbed into French. The French spoken in a dubbed film is usually very clear and precise whereas, with the local product, I often have a great deal of difficulty.

It was thanks to television that I was able to respond positively, albeit untruthfully, to some ladies' questions when I went to buy some tiles at Villegrande Materiaux.

I had chosen my tiles and I went with the lady into the office to conclude the transaction by writing out a cheque.

'*Vous êtes Anglais?*' she asked.

I decided to stretch a point and said yes.

'*Vous habitez Londres?*'

'*Oui*,' I replied stretching another point as I lived some thirty miles from the Capital.

At this juncture the other lady in the office decided to join in the conversation.

'*Vous portez le chapeau melon?*' she asked and burst into peals of laughter.

Now fortunately I had just seen an episode of *The Avengers* on French television which is called *Chapeau Melon et Bottes de Cuir* in France. I knew what she was talking about.

'*Bien sûr,*' I said. '*J'ai deux. Un chapeau melon noir pour le travail et un chapeau melon brun que je porte quand je sors au soir.*'

They were impressed. I was a proper English gentleman.

I have been told that I should have a French TV licence. This came as a bit of a surprise as all the channels have advertisements.

Apparently the French declared an armistice recently for television licence dodgers. Nobody in our village actually turned up to take advantage of the offer. Presumably they were all too busy watching television.

Taff and Melanie are very sociable people. They have a great many visitors to their home in France. Some are unexpected but all are welcome and they enjoy a very high standard of hospitality. Taff is an aficionado of the French sausage and all his house guests will, on at least one occasion, be treated to a sausage barbecue. He will travel to the next village where there is a butcher that produces very superior sausage. Taff will buy a couple of metres which he will wind into a spiral and place on the barbecue. It requires a certain amount of skill to turn the sausage over, without breaking it, when one side is done but Taff is now a master of this art. You can cheat and buy circular sausage holders but there is no fun in that. Endless sausage is a bit like large containers of wine. At the end of the meal you are never quite sure how much you have consumed but you know that it has been a lot.

We are not exactly inhospitable, but our accommodation is limited so I have not broadcast the fact that I have a house in France. Taff, on the other hand has made it known to his wide group of friends that the house is available for their use. This message has travelled far and wide, well beyond his circle of real friends, and it is not unknown for Taff to get a telephone call from an ex-colleague that he has not seen for many years and hardly knew when he did work with him.

If the reunion telephone call starts off, 'Hello old mate,' then Taff knows that it almost certainly concerns the use of his house.

Our guests are mainly family although other friends have used the house from time to time.

We were very surprised that both our daughters liked it so much. The young nowadays always complain of being hard up but they still manage to have at least three holidays a year. Our daughters will go skiing in the early part of the year, visit us in St. Crispin in the summer and go somewhere exotic later in the year.

Both of them have said that their favourite holiday is in St. Crispin. If they could only have a single holiday each year it would in the Languedoc. The strange thing is that their respective husband and boyfriend completely agree.

Charlotte also looks forward to her visits to the South of France as the villagers make such a fuss of her.

They saw her first when she was five weeks old and they have seen her every year since. She is a familiar sight, in her little red Ferrari, pedalling round the village square. We bought her the car one New Year from the local supermarket where it had been reduced to a mere 250 francs. We just left it in the house for her to find when she arrived the next time.

'What a pity it is that we only have one spare bedroom,' Barbara said to me one hot summer's evening.

We were sitting on the terrace at peace with the world. We had eaten out at lunchtime so it was one of our little evening snacks that seemed to go on forever. There was plenty of good fresh bread from the *boulangerie*. There was *pâté* and several types of cheese. There was a green salad and a bowl of the large tasty tomatoes that I call *uglies* because they are so misshapen. There were also peaches and melons which were absolutely delicious and almost given away they were so cheap.

'Charlotte cannot really continue to sleep in the same as room as Vikki and Clive,' she went on.

The arrangement that we had with our children was that we would overlap with them for a week or so then off we would go and leave them on their own for a bit.

'We will just not be able to overlap with them any more,' she concluded.

I looked to see if a tear was running down her cheek but at least she had spared me that.

She knew, and I knew, that there was no way that we would give up our week with Charlotte so I waited for the rest.

'We could always look for a bigger house.'

She had finally said it.

'Just when I have got this one sorted out,' I said.

I did not want to give in too easily. In actual fact I had been thinking along the same lines for a slightly different reason. I had run out of jobs to do when I was on holiday and I was in danger of getting bored.

'OK,' I said, 'I'll go and see Alphonse Pons in the morning.'